Critical Reasoning

By Dr. Robin Roth and Dr. Doug Borcoman

California State University, Dominguez Hills

Copyright © 2010 by Dr. Robin Roth and Dr. Doug Borcoman. All rights reserved. No part of this publication may be reprinted, reproduced, transmitted, or utilized in any form or by any electronic, mechanical, or other means, now known or hereafter invented, including photocopying, microfilming, and recording, or in any information retrieval system without the written permission of University Readers, Inc.

First published in the United States of America in 2010 by Cognella, a division of University Readers, Inc.

Trademark Notice: Product or corporate names may be trademarks or registered trademarks, and are used only for identification and explanation without intent to infringe.

To learn more please visit the website below to access supplementary multimedia presentations based upon the contents of the book.
http://philosophicalquest.org/ct/ct1.html

14 13 12 11 10   1 2 3 4 5

Printed in the United States of America

ISBN: 978-1-935551-97-3

www.cognella.com 800.200.3908

Contents

What is Critical Thinking?	1
Introduction to Philosophical Writing—How to Write a Paper	23
Rhetorical Devices	31
The Voucher System for LA	43
Washington "Health Care"	45
The High and Low Tides of American Education	51

What is Critical Thinking?

By now you have probably heard the term "critical thinking" mentioned frequently in the context of your experience in higher education. Much discussion has taken place among educators, professors and many others regarding how to infuse and incorporate critical thinking into the various disciplines and how to help students such as yourself become better able to use it in their studies as well as in their lives generally.

It is of course important to start your study of critical thinking by attempting to define this, at times, elusive concept. But, where shall we start? The very term suggests that it has something to do with offering a critique or, more simply, a *judgment* about someone or something.

To some extent, that is true. Critical thinking requires at the very least that you exercise judgment about a topic or issue that has come to your attention and that interests you, for one reason or another. But, that is not the whole story. For one thing, when you engage in critical thinking in the philosophical sense, it is very important to remember that you are not judging people. Instead, you are judging or evaluating what another person or group of people *say* or *assert*.

> Here is a philosophical definition of critical thinking offered by some prominent thinkers:
>
> *Critical thinking is the intellectually disciplined process of actively and skillfully conceptualizing, applying, analyzing, synthesizing, and/or evaluating information gathered from, or generated by, observation, experience, reflection, reasoning, or communication, as a guide to belief and action …*

This is where philosophers and other teachers of critical thinking have gotten the idea that this sort of thinking is about *issues* and not about persons, per se. Ideally, when you practice critical thinking you evaluate, critique, analyze, synthesize and clarify the issue that you are dealing with. You attempt to do this without judging the person advocating for or against a particular issue. This means that you do not judge the man, woman, boy, or girl making an assertion of opinion or a statement of belief. Instead, you stay directly *on top of* the topic or issue at hand, trying your best to focus on what is important and not be distracted by what is not important.

Of course, that is the challenge that critical thinking presents to all of us. Think about a recent time when you have argued with someone about an issue that greatly concerns you. It doesn't matter what the issue is. It could be about whether the city you live in should allow unrestricted development. Or, perhaps you feel strongly that recent election results where unreflective of your community's political profile. You try to make your point and the person with whom you are arguing becomes visibly upset and perhaps accuses you of bias or of having a *bad attitude!*

What can, and frequently does, happen in an argument is that the persons involved become frustrated with each other and distracted from the issue at hand to the degree that they fail to stay focused on that issue. In terms of critical thinking, this is a form of *fallacious* reasoning and is one of the many logical fallacies to be identified later in this lesson.

You will now embark upon a kind of journey to discover the important realm of critical thinking. In what follows, you will visit the concept from an historical perspective and ultimately see why fallacious reasoning should be avoided. Moreover, you will learn how to evaluate the claims and positions of others, as well as how to develop a solid argument to support your views and opinions.

A BRIEF HISTORY OF CRITICAL THINKING AND LOGIC

It all started when conscious creatures resembling humans began to ponder how to live, hunt, gather food and defend themselves. This is not to rule out non-humans from the wonderful world of thinking critically. But, as far as we know, it is only human-like, rational beings that have the capacity for reasoning in the way that critical thinking and informal logic require.

In all probability, early humans were accustomed to making inferences about where the best places to live and survive would be, based upon their experiences, perceptions, and accumulated knowledge. As soon as some prehistoric cave dweller began to notice seasonal changes and anticipate changing requirements for shelter, clothing, and comfort, some reflective, intellectual process resembling critical thinking must have begun to kick-in.

Prehistoric critical thinking, at least, would have required that an early human put the proverbial 2 + 2 together to come up with a 4. That being would have reasoned that fire or hot things can cause injury or pain, that certain fruits and grains are ready to be harvested, and that a woman is about ready to have a child. Connections between and among various phenomena would have been observed and our early ancestors would have conducted reasoning about future expectations, at least semi-consciously. In all probability, the better the reasoning on matters such as these, the greater would have been the likelihood of survival!

As humans became more and more self-aware and especially of their thinking processes, they began, at least some of them, to systematize and perfect their reasoning skills. The effort to provide a comprehensive, formal analysis of human reasoning culminated in the work of Aristotle and that of the early Hindus.

What Aristotle in particular did was to provide us with a way to guarantee the results of our reasoning by developing the idea of the *syllogism*. The term syllogism derives from the Classical Greek language and basically means *putting words or sentences together*. So, the idea was to put sentences together in such a way that a conclusion could reasonably and with certainty be inferred from at least two of them.

As the centuries marched on, various thinkers from different cultures contributed to the stockpile of knowledge that was accumulating about logic. Arabic scholars were noteworthy for developing and further systematizing the basic ideas that Aristotle had formulated. Logic was utilized by thinkers such as St. Thomas and Immanuel Kant, both of whom were critical thinkers *par excellence*.

It was in the 19th century that philosophers began to look for connections between the earlier relative of critical thinking and mathematics. This undertaking resulted in what has come to be known as *symbolic logic*. Basically, symbolic logic is a highly structured form of abstract reasoning that resembles mathematics. And, like mathematics, there are many symbols, signs, and rules that need to be mastered in order to complete the required operations.

On the other hand, and you will perhaps rejoice in this, what is now known officially as *critical thinking* or informal logic, does not have the look and feel of mathematics, at all. Primarily a 20th Century phenomenon, the modern idea is that critical thinking provides a practical, hands-on approach to developing and refining your reasoning skills. While this concept evolved from the earlier, historical considerations set forth by previous thinkers about the discipline of logic, it has ended up as a truly *user-friendly* endeavor.

As you will see, if you bear in mind some basic principles of reasoning, namely making inferences, drawing conclusions, and justifying claims, you will be able to apply your native reasoning skills to solving problems and presenting issues. In addition, you will find it possible to apply this form of reasoning to a good many things with which you are already well acquainted.

You will now continue to explore the definition of critical thinking and see why it is important to practice this much needed skill when studying and evaluating important issues that arise in daily life and that are sure to confront you in the new millennium!

MOVING CLOSER TO THINKING CRITICALLY

The modern day philosophers Michael Scriven and Richard Paul have developed a definition of critical thinking that you can apply to your own reflections, discussions, and writing activities. Basically their definition identifies the following skills as essentially part of the concept of critical thinking.

As a critical thinker, you:

- evaluate data
- analyze word meanings
- conceptualize problems
- solve problems
- integrate thinking with behavior
- evaluate claims and arguments

Of course, what you want to add to this list is doing all or most of these things well. In other words, you need to be a good problem solver, a good evaluator of claims and arguments, etc. This means not only practicing these activities but acknowledging the importance of trying to achieve the highest quality when doing critical thinking.

Based upon these elements, you can see that the possibilities for applying critical thinking are limitless. In fact, you are probably doing some serious thinking right now when you try to understand what you are reading at this very moment.

Consider a concrete example of where critical thinking might have come in handy. Think of a time when you tried to convince a friend to see a *good* movie you have been dying to see and you produced an *argument* to convince her/him to see the movie with you.

Perhaps you tried to influence your friend with persuasive tactics or threaten with the possibility that he or she would miss out on an important evening in your company should that person decide not to go. But, this would have been to employ the *fallacy* of *appeal to force or intimidation*, otherwise known as *argumentum ad baculum* or argument by the 'stick.'

> A fallacy occurs whenever there is a distraction or counterfeit claim or reasoning introduced that diverts attention from the real issue. Classic fallacies are: appeal to force, appeal to pity, attacking the person, and slippery slope.

However, if you had consciously sought to convince your audience with well thought out reasoning and then decided carefully to develop a good argument in support of your position, it would at least have been a challenge to your friend to come up with good reasons not to go. This would have gotten you both involved in a discussion about the merits of going to the movie and perhaps even about whether the movie was actually worth seeing.

This means that you would have been doing some or all of the things listed above. The only question would be: did you do them well? In other words, were you avoiding fallacious reasoning and other pitfalls in the course of offering your argument?

In a way, critical thinking is simply thinking seriously, profoundly, reflectively, and consistently about some issue or other. So, it is neither really that mysterious nor unusual, although at times it seems rare to encounter someone who wants seriously to probe more deeply into an issue in order to get beneath the surface and find out what is the most reasonable thing to think or do.

So, as a critical thinker, you would want to substantiate your claim that you should go to the movie by providing reasons, also called *premises* that would serve to convince your listener that you are right.

However, the way in which you succeed in convincing someone of the truth or acceptability of your views on certain matters needs to be looked at carefully. We all need to practice evaluating reasons for claims that we believe are true.

Here's one way to approach building an argument to support your position. Choose reasons or premises that directly relate to your claim and that have factual authenticity. Be sure that you do not *attack* your listener verbally in order to strengthen your point. This is a kind of verbal bullying that does not belong in critical thinking discussions, yet occurs with some frequency in certain arenas, such as politics and talk shows.

> The definition of an argument is a set of statements arranged in such a way that one of them is said to *follow from* the others. The one that follows from the rest is your main claim, otherwise known as the *conclusion*.

When you're satisfied that you have done your best to choose appropriate reasons to justify your position or claim, the next step will be to consciously apply what can be called the "Basic 3" critical thinking method.

THE 3 BASIC COMPONENTS OF CRITICAL THINKING

We would like now to offer you a practical summary of the basic steps to critical thinking. Many writers certainly do have slightly different ways of expressing their views on the subject, but you will find that most of them converge in agreement on these three things: *concept clarification, fact-claim verification, and argument/inference validation.*

These three components, when consciously applied and integrated into your own problem-solving, writing, and meaningful discussion, will help to steer you towards the main objective of critical thinking, namely to clarify and elucidate controversial issues or issues about which there is ongoing disagreement.

Concept clarification is one of the most important aspects in performing well as a thinker. Basically, it involves defining terms and expressions and assuring that there is no ambiguity, vagueness, nor imprecision in a word or term used in an argument.

In the above example, was it clear to you and your friend what a "good movie" is? While there may be quite a bit of disagreement about what constitutes a good movie, discussion about the definition may have helped reduce any misunderstanding likely to have arisen between you.

The second component, namely *fact-claim verification* may require a bit of research on your part. When you attempt to convince someone of the soundness of your viewpoint, it is best to work with believable reasons, that is, those that a reasonable person would judge to be acceptable to common sense. If the issue you have chosen to deal with requires more specialized knowledge, then it is important to provide reference sources such as well-known authorities, professional journals, and dependable web-based resources that are significantly related to the subject.

The last essential element of this process is *argument/inference validation*. What it involves is judging or evaluating the claims and arguments of others in terms of what is known as *argument structure*. This means that you will be looking at the way in which the reasons or premises of an argument provide support for the main claim made by you or another individual.

Getting back, for a moment, to the issue of whether you should have gone to a movie, an example of the kind of reasoning you might have provided is the following:

You say; "We should go to see *Gone With the Wind* because, it is good movie and everyone else in our neighborhood recommends that we go see it."

Argument-inference validation asks us to examine the way in which the reasons you have given provide support for your claim that you should go to see this movie.

All of these components go hand-in-hand when it comes to fully evaluating an argument. However, there is no particular order in which you must do them.

You may now put the 3 components together and evaluate the structure and content of your argument by diagramming it as a simple *syllogism* as in the following:

- Premise 1: *Gone With the Wind* is a good movie.
- Premise 2: Everyone should go to see good movies.
- Conclusion: Therefore, we should go see *Gone With the Wind!*

Notice that you have arranged the previous argument in order easily to tell which statements are premises and which one is the conclusion. Sometimes it is necessary to re-word the original argument slightly without changing the intended meaning. This is the *argument/inference validation* step of critical thinking.

You would next see if the premises are believable, true or factual by asking yourself if there is any further research that you need to do. Also, you would look to see if there are any fallacies present. This is the *fact-claim verification* step.

For example, if one of the premises had been *everyone is going to see Gone With The Wind* this would not be a particularly relevant statement because it exemplifies the fallacy called *appeal to the majority*. It is a fallacy largely because it is not clear that just because everyone is going to see the movie, you should go along with their idea. They all could have poor taste in movies, for all you know!

Lastly, you would evaluate the terms used to determine if a definition is needed for further clarification. This, of course, is the *concept clarification* step of critical thinking. The concept *good movie* may need to be spelled out so that everyone understands the same thing by it and is therefore arguing about the same issue.

You have been given a brief introduction to the useful concept of critical thinking and some fundamental tools that can be used in just about any situation where you find it necessary to support and justify your claims, beliefs, and points-of-view. While there are many textbooks and articles available on this subject that seem to be published almost daily, you have been presented with the *nuts and bolts* of the critical thinking method.

Have you ever felt that you could have made your point with greater clarity or defended your position with more substantial reasons and reasoning? Perhaps you have had an encounter in which you felt that you could have done a better job in presenting the reasons and evidence for your beliefs and opinions. If so, you will probably find that if you pay conscious attention to the manner in which you present your argument by using the *Basic 3* critical thinking method, you will be able to convince others with good reasons and solid reasoning skills.

In addition, we want you to think about how you might be able to apply this method to issues arising in your own life and community, whether at home, school, or in the workplace. Most of us have had many occasions for sharing and expressing our views with others who may agree or disagree with our claims. Sometimes our disagreements can degenerate into heated disputes, frustrated verbal exchanges, and, in extreme cases, noticeable hostility. When this happens, the issue will become clouded and lost in a maze of distractions that lead us away from the core ideas and topics that really concern us.

What we would also wish you to remember is that one of the more important things about the practice of effective thinking skills is separating out what is being said from who is saying it. It is important to take an objective stance towards the claims made by others and to present an attitude of respect to those who make such claims. If someone declares a belief in something that you find, at first, completely disagreeable, stand back for a moment and apply the Basic 3. This will help you to determine if what someone says is worth believing or not because it is well reasoned not because you either like or dislike the person, but because the claim stands up under critical thinking scrutiny.

Alternatively, you have very likely seen an advertisement in which an attractive individual or a well-known celebrity is selling some product allegedly designed to improve your life in some way or another. Instead of finding this person disagreeable, you find her most compelling. Because she looks, speaks, and behaves in manner that you may find irresistible, you pick up the phone and charge your credit card for the *new and improved, automatic abdominal muscle contractor* guaranteed to make your stomach look like a washboard!

In either of these two cases, it is important for you to remember that, ideally, you should have good reasons for buying something, voting for someone, and believing some claim based upon a lucid assessment of the reasons given and the reasoning used and not upon whether the person or organization is attractive, popular, well-known, or even intimidating.

Please be sure to remember the Basic 3 critical thinking components as you navigate through the rest of this workbook. You will discover that one of the keys to unraveling life's important issues is a basic understanding of how to evaluate the reasoning of others who propose and assert certain claims and offer attractive theories.

CRITICAL THINKING AND DISCUSSION

By now you may be asking yourself, "This is fairly interesting, but, how can I use what I have learned so far?" This lesson will attempt to answer that question by introducing you to the philosophical concept of dialogue—that is, deep discussion about important issues in which critical thinking can play a major role.

We will first take a look at a fragment of a dialogue written by the ancient master himself, namely, Plato, to whom you may have been previously exposed. It was Plato, more than anyone else, who took the dialogue form to its highest level in his many written works including the Republic, Euthyphro, Phaedo, and many, many others. Plato portrayed Socrates as the lead character in these written pieces in which he seems to have captured the mood of the conversation and the climate of the times.

You will explore not only the concept of dialogue-discussion, but also the various *kinds* of dialogue that can take place. Moreover, you will also be introduced to a model of communication that many information theorists have employed for the past few decades called the Shannon-Weaver model.

This model attempts to diagram the process of communicating with someone or something and thus serves as a paradigm of what happens between at least two parties where there is an attempt at exchanging or transmitting information or meaning.

Finally, you will learn how to employ a basic technique in dialogue sometimes referred to as the Socratic Method. In this kind of communication the participants are mutually engaged in the exploration of each other's ideas with the hope in mind that they will find deeper understanding and clarity in regard to the topic under discussion.

What I hope you will remember from all of this is that, once again, critical thinking techniques are not restricted to the repertoire of a professional. A philosopher, for example, is someone who is a lover and seeker of wisdom and, as such, is like anyone else who is passionately interested in finding out more about the world and how we think about it. Critical thinking can help all of us in this type of pursuit.

I think you will see that the philosophical spirit of critical thinking very much finds expression in dialogical practice and conversation.

WHAT HAPPENS IN DIALOGUE?

As you might have guessed by now, the philosophical notion of dialogue does differ somewhat from what people ordinarily mean when they use the term in normal parlance.

You have probably participated in an enormous amount of discussions, talks, and casual chats during your lifetime, and have surely observed others doing the same. Have you ever taken a good long look at someone talking with someone else? Have you listened periodically to bits and pieces of their conversation, not in the sense of eavesdropping, but in the sense in which you just happened to be close by and couldn't help but overhear what they had to say to each other—and how they said it?

What do you think is going on? It may be that you have observed or participated in chit-chats wherein you or someone else casually and amicably exchanges information and viewpoints. These can be quite pleasant social events and you may have found that a certain amount of satisfaction can be had from such interactions. But, don't you also find that it is often true that such informal conversations are not intended to go beyond a certain level of involvement or truth-seeking--that is, they are not undertaken with the idea to penetrate deeply beneath the surface, so to speak?

Perhaps you have been a recent participant in a controversial dispute that was not as amicable as the one just mentioned. I would imagine that you found yourself, at times, becoming frustrated with your disputant, maybe even feeling strongly that you wanted to win this verbal battle in order to assure that you have convinced your *opponent* of the correctness of your views and beliefs or of the inadequacy of his or her opinions.

The above scenarios are two distinct kinds of human, verbal interaction and, of course, there are many others. I mention them here only to point out now that philosophical dialogue can resemble these activities but that it generally differs radically with respect to depth of discussion, level of mutual exploration of ideas, and the absence of competitiveness. That is, the idea that you must *win* your arguments and conversations is largely irrelevant in philosophical dialogue.

In other words, to heighten the contrast, philosophical dialogue is a method of communication in which the speakers are on equal terms, listening carefully to each other, evaluating what is said, and being unconcerned about winning or losing. In fact, while a critical thinking dialogue can easily resemble what is called debate, the spirit of such dialogue is one of cooperation.

In debate, for example, the goal is typically, among other things, a competitive one. It is frequently to win an argument. On the other hand, in dialogue, there is a humble attempt to foster mutual respect for each other's ideas and a willingness to admit errors in reasoning as well as to acknowledge mistakenly held beliefs. Remember, such errors in reasoning can often take the form of fallacies and rhetorical devices.

You will now see how to conduct meaningful dialogue first by taking a quick look at a *classic* example!

PLATO—MASTER OF THE WRITTEN DIALOGUE

Plato lived in the 4th Century B.C. in Athens Greece and wrote many dialogues wherein Socrates played the key role. You will now see how a dialogue basically can work in real life after we take a quick look at the somewhat dramatically contrived version of dialogue Plato offers us.

In Plato's work called the *Euthyphro*, pronounced *you-thigh-fro*, Socrates and the character of Euthyphro are talking about the definition of holiness or piety. Euthyphro is an ancient Greek priest and Socrates' intent is to determine whether he really knows what holiness is!

The following excerpt is a translation from the original Greek play by the classicist Benjamin Jowett. I have abbreviated, for convenience, the names of the principal speakers in this dialogue, namely Euthyphro and Socrates. The latter has just asked his fellow speaker to give him a definition of piety or what we usually refer to in our modern world as *holiness*.

Before you take a look at the dialogue, remember that it exemplifies the use of the Socratic Method. In the following dialogue, we begin with Socrates putting a question to his comrade.

This time-honored method of discovering the truth can be boiled down to a deliberate sequence of events that is intended to occur in philosophical dialogue as Socrates envisioned it.

> In the Socratic Method, participants:
>
> 1. Exhibit wonder. A question is posed out of curiosity.
> 2. Form a hypothesis. A reasonable answer is offered.
> 3. "Participate in *elenchus*. Cross-examination by questioning is conducted, and
> 4. Accept the hypothesis as provisionally true.

Perhaps you will notice that the Socratic Method resembles what contemporary thinkers regard often as the *scientific method* in what follows.

THE DIALOGUE

Socrates to Euthyphro: Remember that I did not ask you to give me two or three examples of piety, but to explain the general idea which makes all pious things to be pious. Do you not recollect that there was one idea which made the impious what it is and the pious what it is?

Euth: I remember.

Soc: Tell me what is the nature of this idea, and then I shall have a standard to which I may look, and by which I may measure actions, whether yours or those of any one else, and then I shall be able to say that such and such an action is pious, such another impious.

Euth: I will tell you, if you like.

Soc: I should very much like.

Euth: Piety, then, is that which is dear to the gods, and impiety is that which is not dear to them.

Soc: Very good, Euthyphro; you have now given me the sort of answer which I wanted. But whether what you say is true or not I cannot as yet tell, although I make no doubt that you will prove the truth of your words.

Euth: Of course.

Soc: Come, then, and let us examine what we are saying. That thing or person which is dear to the gods is pious, and that thing or person which is hateful to the gods is impious, these two being the extreme opposites of one another. Was not that said?

Euth: It was.

Soc: And well said?

Euth: Yes, Socrates, I thought so; it was certainly said.

Admittedly, the language is a bit dusty and the manner of speaking a little alien to those of us living in the *new millennium*. But, please do notice that these two speakers are communicating with each other in way that continues the thread of the discussion. Socrates asks a question and Euthyphro answers. Then, Socrates advances a conception of what he has in mind about standards or definitions. In short, there is an agreement between the two speakers to interact positively and to keep the discussion moving along. One statement or question made by one participant leads to a response or a clarification made by the other.

Let us now see how this pattern of communicative interaction called dialogue can be applied to a more current, less distant-seeming issue, such as the controversial idea that certain non-human animals, such as dolphins, have rights. I will create two characters here and set-up a conversation on this issue so that you can see how a philosophical dialogue can begin to take shape.

Here is the scenario: Two college students at an imaginary campus, call it *Atypical-U*, just left a lecture in which the presenter made some unusual claims about the moral rights of animals. Basically, the presenter thinks that it makes sense to talk of the rights of certain other species. The first student, Homer, thinks the idea that animals other than humans could have rights is preposterous, while the second student, Pandora, believes that the idea makes good sense.

> **Homer:** What that lecturer said was completely beyond comprehension. Humans are the only beings that could meaningfully have rights.
>
> **Pandora:** I know that it seems strange to talk of other animals having rights, but the lecturer did say that, by definition, anything that is a *person* can be said to have rights. Humans are obviously persons and perhaps dolphins are, but less obviously, persons also.
>
> **Homer:** Well, Pandora, I grant you that it makes sense to think that a person has rights. But, my problem is, I don't think anything other than a human could be a person. Perhaps we can define the term *person* so I can get a better handle on what the real issue is.
>
> **Pandora:** Good idea. Let me start! A person is something that is self-aware, thinks rationally, and can experience pleasure and pain.
>
> **Homer:** Okay. That's a nice starting place. Let's examine this concept and see if any of the characteristics you have just now mentioned might not always apply. In fact, maybe there are a few others we should also consider.
>
> **Pandora:** Yes—I think we can add to our list.

Here you have two persons attempting to disclose their ideas to each other and neither of them seems to be trying to outdo the other. They are both looking cooperatively at an interesting issue and appear to be off to a good start in their mutual pursuit of discovering what each other thinks and believes about this issue.

TWO MODELS OF COMMUNICATION

I now turn your attention to a modern way of illustrating what happens ultimately in communication through dialogue first by way of the Shannon-Weaver model of communications.

Fig. 1. *The Shannon-Weaver Model*

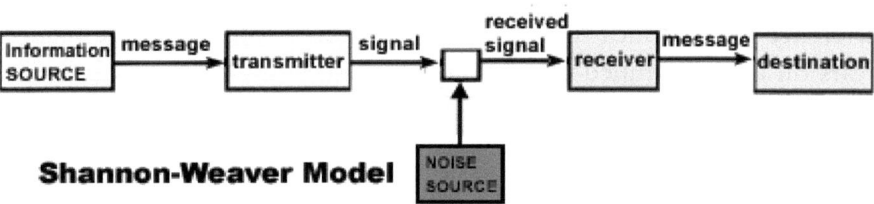

This model is used by information theorists to help us get an idea about the process of communication taking place between a sender and a receiver. It helps us to see the basic components of information exchange, such as that occurring in a broadcast announcement transmitted over the radio. However, it falls short when it comes to capturing truly what happens in dialogue.

If you focus on what ideally should happen in communication between two speakers when everything goes well, you will observe the following. If communication is to be successful then the "dialoguers" must be alert and aware, paying careful attention to what each other says as well as assuring that the *channel* stays tuned-in. This means that participants concentrate their attention on the information being transmitted and are receptive to the *process* of communication and dialogue as it progresses.

This is why the following diagram helps to enhance the Shannon-Weaver model, giving us a more accurate illustration of communication through dialogue.

Fig. 2.1 *Thou Communications Model*

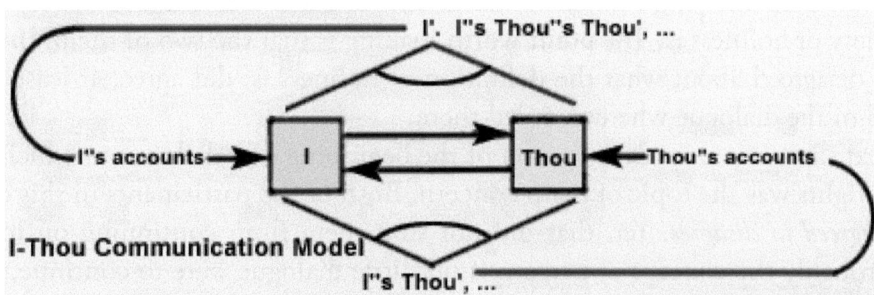

Dialogue, itself, unlike other forms of communication, stresses the *bi-directional* nature of the flow of meaning and information. Unlike TV, radio, or listening to a lecture for the most part, dialogue is a two-way street. Philosophical dialogue, then, is a two-way street in which there is much questioning and answering and a sustained effort made by all parties to continuously promote this activity until clarification and understanding are reached. And this is best done through the use of critical thinking.

As a participant in a dialogue, you therefore not only listen attentively to what is being said, that is the *message*, but you think about it seriously in order to respond with an answer and a question of your own. If you don't understand what has been said, then you ask for clarification in order carefully to evaluate the information presented to you.

There are times when what is referred to as *white noise* can creep into a dialogue and cause interference with an idea that someone expresses. Rather like the *snow* that sometimes appears on a poorly tuned-in television station, white noise can prevent you from understanding the point that someone wishes to make. In other words, you cannot clearly make out what the other person means. Sources of this type of interference are frequently *internally generated* and are the consequences of not listening carefully, letting personal bias affect your judgment of another point-of-view, or being distracted by other unrelated thoughts and issues.

To clear up the noise, it is often helpful to ask a few questions for clarification of intended meaning and to repeat in your own words your understanding of what the other person seems to be saying. To do this is to engage in a form of active listening in which you are consciously attempting to understand what is being said in order to further the dialogue process.

To sum up, if things go well in a dialogue, you will be approaching deeper and deeper levels of meaning and insight as your ideas spiral into those of the others in your dialogue, as diagram 2, above, illustrates. When this happens, you end up learning much more, not only about the issue under discussion, but also a lot more about—yes—yourself!

CONCLUSION

We have looked at a classic Platonic dialogue in which Socrates attempted to *pick the brain* of a contemporary of his named Euthyphro. In the full version of the dialogue, Socrates ultimately ends up showing his friend that neither of them seems to have a very good idea of what piety or holiness is. The point worth making is that the two of them, though they may have disagreed about what the definition of holiness is, did agree, at least, to follow the thread of the dialogue wherever it led them.

You next saw a more modern version of the beginning of a dialogue in which the issue of animal rights was the topic of main concern. Both of the participants in this discussion basically *agreed to disagree*. Yet, that did not stop them from continuing on to examine more thoroughly the concept of person. If our little dialogue were to continue, I am sure that you would see it culminate in a deeper understanding of animal rights and of personhood in the minds of both of the dialoguers.

The communication models offered here can help you to understand, in diagram form, the basic process that occurs when meaning or information is successfully transferred from a source, such as a person, to a target, such as a radio receiver, another person, or possibly your laptop computer. The basic, so called *Shannon-Weaver* model (Fig.1) seems to provide a good way of understanding the process of *data transmission and reception* such as that which happens when your computer modem communicates with a remote server on the Internet.

The second model presented (Fig. 2) seems more appropriate for *human* communication especially with respect to the use of critical thinking during discussion. When such dialogue is sustained for a period of time, there is a kind of interpenetration of beliefs and ideas that actually goes beyond mere two-way communication. What can happen is that ideas cross-pollinate as persons engaged in dialogue continue their pursuit of truth, clarification, and self-knowledge. And, the consequence of cross-pollination is often times a new, hybrid idea formed from this type of philosophically deep discussion between two or more human beings.

Now here are a few ideas for you to contemplate. The first one is that you can incorporate critical thinking skills into your conversations. Socrates did this when he drew inferences and developed conclusions from what others said in the course of discussion. He then, of course, subsequently revealed the inconsistent beliefs and opinions held by most of his fellow interlocutors.

Next, critical thinking discussion is really more an art of communication than it is a science. That is why there really is no recipe that you can follow, except to note that skillful questioning and a willingness to follow questions and answers logically where they might lead conduces to a deeper, richer dialogue experience.

Finally, when undertaken seriously and responsibly, genuine philosophical dialogue can foster a sense of intellectual community, a commitment to honest disclosure of opinions and beliefs, and ultimately a feeling of openness to new possibilities and paradigms.

Being open to the possibilities afforded by critical thinking is what makes old ideas seem forever new!

THE SCIENTIFIC METHOD

Have you every thought that the 21st century environment in which we live is one in which you could say that *science makes the world go around?* We all rely upon the research efforts of scientists working together from around the world to solve such problems as disease, excessive population growth, crop failure, organ replacement, and many, many others.

We even enjoy the luxury of those *scientific* measures that are taken to make us all look better and become more attractive by having tighter abs, fresher breath, and access even to a chemical means to arouse and stimulate those whom we are trying to impress.

As an example of the latter, we caught an advertisement recently on local television that was promoting the use of a chemical food supplement that would attract members of the opposite sex.

According to this ad, all you need do is to pay your *$39.95*, take the required pill twice a day and before you know it, the *object* of your desire will come knocking at your door immediately ready for an evening of romancing, dancing, and cavorting in a dimly lit room.

Complete with diagrams of the human brain, pictures of neural pathways that lead to the thalamus, and a chart of sophisticated-looking research results, this televised ad presented everything it could in a *scientific* fashion.

The inference you obviously are to make is that dependable methods have been utilized to develop a product that is based upon a scientific view of how people are attracted to each other. Just pop a few pills and the fruits of such research methodology will be yours for the taking!

I am sure that you may be telling yourself right now that you would not be tricked into purchasing such a product even if the promised results appear to be well-supported by scientific-looking research. But, what rational grounds do you have for not believing the claims made by a company or organization, bolstered as they are by an appeal to a methodology that looks, on the face of it, like a scientific one?

We would like to take you on a very brief tour of the world of scientific method as well as explore the critical thinking orientation that justifies and sustains this method. You will also take a look at some of the early and modern western thinkers who started to develop and practice this current way of operating within and thinking about our world.

Since it is important to distinguish between genuine science and what can be referred to as *pseudoscience*, or false science, this lesson will also briefly delve into those regions of controversy that stir up that sort of debate.

In particular you will take a longer look at the issue of whether or not there is a scientific basis for thinking that a certain chemical ingredient causes others to find you more attractive!

You will also see how critical thinking in the context of the philosophy of science can help you to assess and evaluate the claims that both scientists and "pseudo scientists" are likely to make.

At least one practical result from this study will be to help us all answer the question about whether or not the above ad truly utilized genuine scientific methods in order to justify its conclusion about the product offered for sale.

THE SCIENTIFIC METHOD

You have already seen how the philosopher Socrates used the Socratic Method in dialogue to engage his colleague in a discussion about the definition of holiness. This method represents a sustained effort at arriving at a well-reasoned conclusion about a topic of concern to the participants in the dialogue.

As pointed out previously, the Socratic Method is very similar to the scientific method in that the process of *finding the truth* utilizes an identifiable series of steps in order to discover the facts or, to put the matter differently, to generate true claims that participants can mutually discuss and investigate.

However, what is somewhat different is that the scientific method proceeds by using a wide-ranging collection of systematic observations that help either to corroborate statements made about the world or to disconfirm those statements.

Science also engages in a considerable amount of experimentation. So, it is generally true that the scientist will spend quite a bit more of her time collecting data and conducting experiments whereas Socrates—like someone engaged in philosophical dialogue—would not participate in the experimental aspect nearly as much nor in quite the same way.

I would like you to take a look at what is generally viewed by contemporary thinkers as the basic steps of the modern scientific method. It is important for you to remember, at this point, that this method represents a paradigm or model of discovery and is the historical result of centuries of refinement and analysis.

It is quite reasonable to say that most cultures throughout the world have used some form of the scientific method and have thus helped to contribute to the evolutionary development of this concept.

The steps utilized in the scientific method are:

Observation: This first step occurs when an observation or eye-witness account, is made about some event, thing, or characteristic of the world. Normally, this will lead to a question that stimulates further curiosity and wonder.

Using our previous example, you may have observed that other people seem to be more attracted to you when you have eaten certain foods. This can lead you to ask one of the following questions: *Why does eating certain foods cause other people to be more interested in me? Or what ingredients or chemicals in the food I regularly eat seem to induce this behavior in others?*

Developing a hypothesis: When a scientist attempts to answer a question, she will form a provisional hypothesis or an *educated guess* about the answer. In the example above, there are quite a few hypotheses that could be given, but one promising one might be that certain foods contain ingredients that stimulate the behavior regularly observed.

Experimentation: It is in this area that science distinguishes itself from the other disciplines since a scientist will need to design an experiment or set of experiments to test the hypothesis.

If you were scientifically to figure out why you seem to be more attractive to others after you have ingested certain foods, the challenge to you would be to design an experiment based upon your hypothesis and that is where the real work for the scientist truly begins.

Now that you have a good idea not only of what the scientific method is, but also how it compares to the Socratic Method, you will see how philosophy and science have shared a common historical origin as you move on to the next chapter.

THALES: AN EARLY PHILOSOPHER-SCIENTIST

In the Western tradition, the person credited with taking a giant leap forward in terms of initiating and developing the scientific approach, is the Greek philosopher Thales (thay-leez) of Miletus, who lived in the 6th century B.C.

Thales was a man of many talents. What should be of chief interest to you is that he is probably the first known thinker to break away from the explanatory tradition of his day. That tradition was one in which mythological explanation played a large role in providing an account of how and why the observed events in our world actually take place.

So, for example, the early Greeks of Thales' era would have sought explanations for various visible phenomena such as floods, wars, and disease, by appealing to the invisible *will of the Olympian gods*.

In fact, you may see examples of the *supernaturalistic* approach to explanation in Homer's Odyssey. In this story, the reasons given for warfare, storm, and strife frequently involve reference to the will of Zeus, Athena, or Hera. Any one of these gods or goddesses may be having a *bad hair* day and thus be prone to expressing his or her wrath through the agency of Mother Nature!

So, the philosopher-scientist Thales was struck by the inadequacy of explanations involving supernatural and unobservable or invisible causes. There was no way to confirm or disconfirm any of the claims made about what the gods were allegedly doing behind the scenes. So, everything that took place in the lives of women and men seemed to be due to the unpredictable whims of unseen, hidden personalities.

Thales thus developed a different perspective in which observed events could be explained primarily in terms of observable phenomena in what is now known as *naturalistic explanation*.

This new insight ultimately led to the development of modern science and the scientific method and represents what can be called a *paradigm shift* with respect to how human beings acquire knowledge of the world.

It is, in other words, a *philosophical* orientation to the study of the world that prescribes the steps to take to gain *scientific* knowledge.

GALILEO: A RENAISSANCE PHILOSOPHER-SCIENTIST

As you move up from the ancient period several centuries to the time of Galileo, you will see that Thales' new perspective influenced this Renaissance thinker's study of falling objects. Observing that heavy objects fall with increasing speed, Galileo formulated the hypothesis that speed is directly proportional to the distance traveled by the falling body.

Being unable to verify this hypothesis directly, Galileo deduced the conclusion that objects falling unequal distances require the same amount of elapsed time. But, this is known to be false, so the original hypothesis had to be revised to say, instead, that the speed attained is directly proportional to the time elapsed, not the distance traveled.

From this hypothesis, Galileo was able to infer that the distance traveled by a falling object is proportional to the square of the time elapsed. He then went on to verify this experimentally by rolling balls down an inclined plane. Of course, from that moment forward, the name Galileo became a household word!

We hope you can see that science relies heavily upon observation, questioning, expressing curiosity, developing a hypothesis, and testing the hypothesis all of which work together to create the scientific method.

Add to these things the fact that there is a context or intellectual framework provided by a philosophical insight or paradigm, such as Thales's emphasis upon observation and naturalistic explanation, and you will begin to see the close relationship between science and philosophy.

KUHN: A CONTEMPORARY PHILOSOPHER-SCIENTIST

Where science meets philosophy is in the work of contemporary philosopher of science Thomas Kuhn who authored the revolutionary work in 1962 entitled *The Structure of Scientific Revolutions*. In this ground-breaking work, Kuhn borrows the Greek term *paradigm* and uses it to refer to the set of beliefs or the intellectual framework that scientists work within as they conduct their scientific endeavors.

Kuhn's controversial idea in essence is that science itself does not progress scientifically. Instead, old paradigms change or give way to new ones oftentimes for no particularly good scientific reason. World views change along with philosophical intuitions and insights, thus giving rise to new paradigms and scientific understandings.

What we want you to ponder is the notion that the scientific method has emerged out of one or so of many paradigms and while it, indeed, has been quite successful, this method is not necessarily the only way to gain knowledge about the world.

THE DIFFERENCE BETWEEN SCIENCE AND PSUEDOSCIENCE

A pseudoscientific theory may be characterized as a set of ideas or claims put forth as scientific when they are not.

In other words, while the theory offered has the appearance of a *scientific* theory, it is lacking in one or more important ways and thus fails to meet the modern criteria that would ordinarily apply.

In addition to utilizing the scientific method, a scientific theory should exemplify the following elements. In other words, a good theory should:

a. be based upon empirical observation
b. explain a range of observable phenomena
c. be empirically testable in some meaningful way
d. be confirmed by experiments or with the discovery of new facts
e. be objective and testable by anyone
f. be approached with skepticism rather than gullibility

What frequently happens, as I am sure you have noticed on occasion, is that theories about how we think, learn, become lean, or about how you can make yourself more attractive become popularized in the media.

Because of their initial plausibility, these theories can help to sell you on the desirability of a product or service. Perhaps this is one reason why companies seem to be flourishing on TV and on the Internet—people watching or listening to the commercials are persuaded by the *scientific look* of the evidence and by the personal testimonials delivered via their TV screens or computer monitors!

This brings us back to what might be suspicious about the advertisement I have been mentioning. While it has been presented to the audience as a scientific breakthrough, there is no justification for purchasing the product advertised based upon the rationale presented.

There is neither a disclosed methodology, such as empirical observation, nor corroborated testing of the claim that special chemicals ingested in a food supplement will result in increased attractiveness. All that is offered is a set of charts and illustrations depicting centers of brain activity and associated neural pathways.

What are presented on behalf of the product are testimonials. Yes, plenty of testimonials. How often have you seen an alleged user of a product testify before a camera or in an interview about how she or he benefited significantly from using it? When you think about it, does that alone constitute a good reason for you strongly to consider buying and using the product?

The use of testimonials in this case is a diversion that distracts you from the fact that a scientifically sound theory has not been offered in support of the pseudoscientific claims presented.

Testimonials have almost no value in establishing the likelihood of the truth of these claims and yet are persuasive enough to convince some viewers to *make that call* and order the product. Nevertheless, they are of no more value in this case than would be the televised accounts of satisfied customers of the latest weight loss program.

CONCLUSION

We are quite sure that you have been exposed regularly to the tactics engaged in by advertisers to get you to buy their miracle products. Using pseudoscience to accomplish that end is one of the more elaborate ways in which manufacturers attempt to convince by overwhelming you with scientific-looking *research findings*.

If this tactic works at all, it is probably because most of us are favorably disposed to thinking both of science and the scientific method as extremely successful and reliable means of finding out more about the world and helping us live within it.

But, do you think that the early philosopher-scientists, such as Thales, would have been tricked by these tactics? How about Galileo? Would he have sent a fleet-footed messenger to purchase this product because of the allegedly involved science?

Do you think that either of them would have approved of using science or distorting the scientific method to accomplish these ends?

It seems quite reasonable to say that an appropriate response to many of these pseudo-scientific theories and claims is the Socratic one, namely, to practice a healthy skepticism and to be astutely watchful when *the truth-seeking is mixed with profit-seeking*.

Somewhere along the line, it seems, the truth becomes contaminated when *science* is used to sell products or reinforce a biased belief as opposed to discovering facts about the world.

We have now explored the theme of what constitutes science and how it contrasts with pseudoscience. We have observed the relationship between philosophy and science with respect to the Socratic and scientific methods. By doing so, you are probably realizing that there are, indeed, some important features shared by both. One extremely important feature is: critical thinking

We would like now to stress some important differences between the two. Firstly, although science as we know it came to us primarily by way of philosophy, science is not identical to philosophy. The latter is more general and less-inclined to commit itself to a single method of finding the truth.

On the other hand, as has been discussed, science has adopted the scientific method and has become a widely-accepted framework for understanding the Universe in terms of that method and of commonly accepted principles of theory construction.

Philosophy, it can be said, is not quite so *locked in*. The pursuit of philosophy still leaves it an open question as to whether the scientific method is the only or the best way to conduct the search for the truth or the finding of fact. Philosophers employ critical thinking to help them evaluate this question.

Because it is more generalized, or at least more abstract, the practice of philosophy allows us to *go behind the scenes* of a scientist's thinking to unravel the biases, beliefs, methodologies and intellectual commitments that the scientist herself may be unaware of. We use critical thinking in order to help us perform that task.

Probably the best way to put it is that philosophers examine the scientific paradigms or cognitive models that are utilized in the practice of science. They are thus able to discover what are the assumptions, biases and beliefs latent in a scientific *world-view*. And that is part of what we do to ourselves when we engage in critical thinking.

By doing so, all of us can develop great insight into the systems of knowledge and belief acquisition and determine the extent to which scientific (and other) belief systems might impact how we see the world.

The philosopher-critical thinker takes a step back and says: *Is this the only way to view the world?* In that sense, even someone normally viewed primarily as a scientist, namely Albert Einstein, was actually a philosopher because his famous *Theory of Relativity* was primarily a response to this question.

Introduction to Philosophical Writing— How to Write a Paper

Have you ever found yourself deeply interested in some subject that came up in conversation or appeared in a television broadcast? Have inspired thoughts occurred to you that you later wished you had written down? Have you wondered about what might have happened had you taken the time to record some of these spontaneous insights?

We would now like to introduce you to the importance of journal writing to philosophy. In fact, you will be introduced to this relevant topic by starting a journal of your own once you have learned about the process and how to keep a record of your thoughts and ideas. Writing a journal can help you develop your thoughts and insights in order to allow you greater access to your *self*.

In addition, you will be presented with some tips on writing another kind of work, namely a philosophical essay. This kind of project includes an element of argumentation wherein you propose and defend your own views on matters that have philosophical significance. You will see that a journal can complement an essay by helping you to clarify and expand your own ideas.

This information should help you whenever it becomes necessary to substantiate a belief or opinion, justify a claim or conclusion, and convince someone of the correctness of your view or position on a subject.

What you should bear in mind is that philosophical writing is done in light of the concept of critical thinking that was introduced in the previous sections. So, even though a journal is usually thought of as less formal and not as rigorous as a research paper, your writing should still reflect the skills of making inferences and drawing conclusions about matters of interest to you.

It can be said that one of the purposes of a philosophical journal is to provide a means to discuss and explore your own thinking on a variety of philosophical issues in a less formal manner than would be expected were you asked to write an argumentative essay or research paper.

This means that writing a philosophical journal differs from other kinds of writing primarily because you will have a certain freedom to pursue many ideas rather than developing a continuous line of argument or exposition on one particular topic.

Also, unlike a research paper, you are not expected to generate a bibliography of research materials, although you may refer to news reports, magazine articles, talk show programs and discussions that you have had in the course of writing and reflecting upon your ideas.

What I believe you will discover is that a journal can be a very good way of brainstorming your ideas on concepts and issues before you actually sit down to write up a more *official* proposal or argument paper.

Consequently, you will also be able to see that philosophical journal keeping and argument paper writing are, while distinct activities, related to each other and mutually beneficial.

WHAT IS A PHILOSOPHICAL JOURNAL?

A journal can be regarded as a method of thinking out loud or carrying on a dialogue with your *self* through writing. The different entries you make in a journal express your observations, thoughts, feelings and experiences in a journey of self-discovery.

Journal remarks and entries bring you into closer contact with the ideas behind an article in a book or magazine or an idea or observation you may have had. The process of journal writing takes you to a deeper and richer understanding of the issues you are dealing with.

Journal writing may be about a course you are taking, a book you are reading, or even about the many insights you have had while driving on the freeway!

The University of Oregon Philosophy Department has rightly published the following in reference to journal writing:

A journal can be a way to:

- Reflect on new ideas or insights that you have.
- Elaborate on some aspects of the course content or class discussion.
- Engage in a critique of reading and conversation about reading assignments.
- Integrate your education by making connections between your courses, and between your course and your lived experience.
- Express aesthetic or artistic impressions of the course content.
- Formulate questions about the reading.
- Analyze the central argument in the reading.

What we would like you to add to this list is using critical thinking skills in order to develop your own thinking and to evaluate it honestly and thoughtfully.

Since writing a journal is taking a kind of journey of discovering who you are, there is also an element of what can be called *self-discovery* writing. This type of writing is designed to help you to develop deeper insight into various matters by identifying, clarifying, and elaborating your beliefs.

As an example, you may have a strong feeling that watching television is actually detrimental to original thinking. There are those who do think this and have offered their reasoning, research, and evidence to support this position. However, since you are not developing a research project when you write a journal, what you would do in this case is to begin documenting your thoughts on television watching on a regular basis. You would be using your own *first person* observations as a starter.

You begin by making an entry, dating it, then writing your initial thoughts and observations down. Perhaps the process would begin like this:

> *Dec. 25th: Today I watched an **infomercial** that seemed to be telling me that in order to have friends and be successful, I must have whiter teeth. Various people were depicted in this advertisement, all of whom were reasonably attractive, in apparently good physical shape, and with very white teeth! I wonder if it is really true that having white teeth is important. It certainly does seem to me that the message here is to buy the product that is being promoted, almost as if to say that I can't function properly without it.*

Your next entry might then look like this:

> *Dec. 27th: I have been thinking a lot about how important white teeth are to being popular and having meaningful relationships. My friends don't seem to be worried too much about the brightness of my teeth and it is hard for me to imagine that it would make a significant difference to my loved ones if I went out and purchased the product to make them glisten. I am also wondering about how television is able to be so persuasive about what I should look like and more importantly, who I should be.*

I hope that you can see how this *thought thread* can be continued almost indefinitely. The next step would be to identify the philosophical motifs and to evaluate the subject-matter using many, if not all, of the journal skills mentioned above.

ADDING CONTENT TO YOUR JOURNAL

As you continue to add threads to your journal, you will find that this form of *self-discovery* writing may result in asking deeper philosophical questions about yourself. When you regularly document your reflections, you may come to realize that your own beliefs may need further evaluation and clarification. This can be a positive sign of making progress on your own unique journey.

Honest and deliberate self-reflection is one of the most daunting philosophical activities that you can become involved in. Writing a journal can be therefore both demanding and rewarding, at the same time, and one key to successful self-discovery is mastery of the skill of forming meaningful questions.

Return, for a moment, to our TV infomercial example. I may wish to continue my *journaling* by adding another entry, such as:

*Jan 1st: It is the first of the year—a time for making resolutions and pondering ways to improve myself, my life and, in some small way, the world. In thinking about whiter teeth, I have come to the realization that much of what we do to or for ourselves has to do with appearance. I mean, whether it is having whiter teeth, a slender, lean stomach, or driving a new SUV, it all seems to boil down to **having** as opposed to just **being**.*

*What I think I mean is what Socrates must have had in mind when he said **The unexamined life is not worth living**. If I interpret this correctly, he is suggesting that we should all take a long look at what we are, what we have, and what meaning there is associated with our lives. Do I become a better, more fulfilled person because I use a product that will whiten my smile? Will others find me more amicable or of greater worth because I purchased and use an abdominal exerciser?*

There are a few deeper levels of philosophical journal writing that I would like you to consider. The example above is indicative of someone beginning to think a little more seriously about what he or she has been asked to purchase and what philosophical implications this may have for the buyer.

Another level of journal writing involves a focused effort to identify and explore various levels of one's own beliefs. In this case, you would show how different beliefs are connected and then draw some conclusions from your observations. This contrasts with efforts made by writers who simply perform the process of self-reflection since the more advanced journal writer expects to draw conclusions about the activity of connecting ideas in the form of what is referred to as *constructed knowledge*.

> The concept of constructed knowledge develops the idea that you design and create, to some extent, your own knowledge –base without ignoring the critical thinking process.

Lastly, an advanced journal writer continues the path of self examination but with greater focus on metacognitive processes that involve asking questions about how we think and how we construct our worlds of belief and knowledge. As such a writer, you would provide readers with insight into the analysis of key concepts and arguments, frequently using the critical thinking concepts presented previously.

Ultimately, a journal is about and for you. It is a record of your navigation through the realm of ideas and, in that regard, is much like a ship's log in which a journey is recorded and documented. You can go back at any time and take another look at your reflections and how you charted your course through the territory of ideas and concepts.

WRITING A PHILOSOPHY PAPER

When you sit down to write a philosophy paper you may discover that it is difficult, at first, to decide upon a topic to write on. This is not unusual. It is quite normal to be puzzled over what to write about, let alone, how to write about it. Obviously, writer's block can affect us all and, in the case of writing a philosophy paper, the blockage can come from several sources. Not the least of which is the fact that philosophy is, by its very nature, a puzzling and perplexing undertaking to begin with!

So, the first thing to bear in mind is to pick a topic. You might find it useful to pore over your journal and see what theme has interested you the most. Then, go with that one. One of the most important and overlooked rules of thumb is, when possible, to select a topic that actually *excites* you. If you can manage to find some idea, concept, or argument that is, for some reason, already appealing to you, you will find that writing about it will not be so painful nor so difficult to undertake.

Secondly, once you have selected a topic, narrow it down so that you can be very specific about what you wish to write on. A 2-5-page paper, for example, on the philosopher Socrates cannot possibly do justice to that topic, nor to him, because there are just too many things to say about Socrates. Focusing upon a specific argument that Socrates advanced or elaborating upon some theme or statement of his that you are interested in would be more realistic. If you eventually decide to take another philosophy course, I can almost guarantee that your instructor will require at least one paper and she will want to see that you are quite clear on what you are trying to state as well as on the conclusion you are attempting to draw.

Basically, the sort of philosophy paper you will likely write can be called an *argument/ analysis* essay in which you will try to:

a) define a concept and/or state a thesis or position,
b) argue for or against a specific position or criticize and evaluate a given concept,
c) defend your argument, reasoning or evaluation with solid (and sound) reasoning methods, and
d) reach a conclusion concerning your position or concerning the analysis of the chosen topic or concept.

Your paper should also reflect the use of critical thinking and problem-solving skills, particularly those we highlighted in the last section. This is why it is important to have a basic grasp of the relevant concepts so that you will be better able to substantiate and justify your essay's main thesis.

To make the writing process, at least in its preliminary phases, relatively neat and clean, I recommend that you employ what can be called the *3T* method. This method provides a convenient way to organize your thoughts while at the same time giving you the opportunity to stay focused and remain consistent in the writing of your essay.

The 3T method in essence provides you with the basic architecture of an essay. The first T stands for *Tell us what you are going to do*. The second T stands for simply *Tell us* while the third T stands for *Tell us what you did*.

Now this may not sound very profound, but the 3T method keeps reminding you of what you are doing, which is basically justifying your claim. If you continually ask yourself, as you develop and write your essay, what am I trying to say?, am I saying it?, and did I succeed in saying it?, you have a better chance of staying focused on your topic. Indeed, these are the 3 main things that the method discloses to you.

Try to put this in the context of a standard written essay in which there is normally an introductory section, main body, and conclusion. What the 3T method does, in conjunction with standard essay structure, is to make you self-consciously aware of whether or not you are sticking to the topic you first selected. This is very important when it comes to writing philosophy papers because you are after consistency, clarity, and coherence, not to mention some critical thinking applied throughout.

We would like now to wrap up this all up by providing you some final tips on organizing an outline for writing a more *formal* essay. This should give you some guidance as you ponder what you need to accomplish when you attempt to apply critical thinking to the writing process.

THE 3 T METHOD FOR WRITING A PAPER

First T *State the proposition to be proved or concept to be analyzed. This is the first T of the 3T method, otherwise known as the introduction.*

In the first, introductory paragraphs of your essay specifically indicate what topic will be examined or discussed. It is often a good idea to report or summarize what other writers, such as philosophers, have said about your chosen topic. Then, introduce to the reader exactly what claim you are trying to prove or justify. One way to do this is to state as tersely as possible in a single sentence what you are *going to do*. An example would be: *In this essay I shall show that television ads present an unreal picture of what it means to be a happy person.*

So, here, you briefly state your reasons for the position you are defending on this issue.

Second T *Give the argument for your position that is, for the claim you are trying to justify. This is the second T of the 3T method, otherwise known as the main body.*

This is where the critical thinking elements mentioned already begin to kick in. You would now use argument/inference validation, fact/claim verification, and concept clarification in order to establish your point in further detail. Remember that this basically means that you would be working to develop a good argument, with factual premises and clearly defined terms and expressions. In a standard 5-8 page essay, this part would normally require you to develop about 3 or so paragraphs.

Third T   *Present the conclusion of your essay's argument. This is the third T and is otherwise known as; you guessed it, the conclusion.*

At this point, you concisely restate your argument in brief-final comments. In the terminology of the 3T method, you are now *telling us what you have done*. This means that you will write a summary paragraph that, in essence, resembles your introductory paragraphs. That is, you have begun your essay and concluded it, remaining steadfastly on the topic you selected all throughout.

Please notice that, by following this brief outline and incorporating the 3T elements, you are assuring the use of critical thinking techniques and also making it quite clear that you have remained on task and focused on the subject you intended to deal with. One of the biggest problems that philosophical writers have is staying on course and not veering away from where they originally intended to go.

To recap, the journal writing process is more flexible, usually more introspective, and allows you to delve deeply into your beliefs, attitudes and assumptions in an informal way. In contrast, a philosophical essay is a more structured, more formal pursuit and possesses the kind of architecture that has been outlined in the 3T method.

Both of these activities, while distinct, are complementary. The writer who navigates through the reflective waters of deep thinking in her journal will have far more success in determining what to write about, and what to write, in her philosophical essay or argument paper.

More on this and other critical thinking themes can be found at our companion website: http://philosophicalquest.org/ct/ct1.html

Rhetorical Devices

PERSUASION THROUGH RHETORIC

- If you like reading, writing—or listening—you will love this.

What we have to say is sometimes important—but the words we use to say what we are thinking are also important. Language is not always neutral. Language can be persuasive. Language affects our thinking, attitudes, beliefs, and behavior —positively or negatively.

Language is powerful.

If language were not so powerful—then dictators like Mussolini or Hitler would not have bothered to go to such great lengths to control it.

Or again, the way we use language can reinforce sexism, racism, nationalism, bigotry and prejudices. It can bias us. Language has a huge influence over us. So we first need to appreciate the power of language in our lives. Be aware of language for all thinking has aspects of linguisticality.

Accepting that, we now want to investigate some of the ways language can affect us. We all know people swear—for effect. And people use language to lie, manipulate, con, hedge, hint, joke, invoke, etc.

Words have rhetorical force or rhetorical meanings.

Words have enormous persuasive power. Their power effects our emotions, images, attitudes, and actions.

Rhetoric refers to the study of persuasive writing. Aristotle, the Ancient Greek philosopher, wrote about rhetoric. Today, Aristotle's works are still used in Critical Thinking and English writing classes as well as in film script and play writing courses. Rhetoric, effectively, has many uses. A good writer can use rhetoric to create moods, humor, anger, fear, or to deceive. Hence, it is important that you recognize rhetorical devices.

Because rhetorical devices are rather common place there is a list of many of them that you will need to know. Recognizing rhetorical devices—not to mention learning how to use them—will take practice, reading, and thinking. You are probably already familiar with some—as they are so often used and mentioned in books, articles, TV shows, and radio talk shows. Rhetorical devices are very useful too. They can be used in arguments, employed by exceptionally good writers of both fiction and non-fiction, and they can be used in propaganda or advertising. Rhetorical devices can move us to action, inspire us, bias us, and entertain us.

Remember, rhetorical devices affect you positively or negatively and they can be used for good or bad purposes.

Further, as Critical Thinkers, we must be able to distinguish between a genuine, logical, cogent arguments and things that are written or said rhetorically, which have psychological but not logical force.

Rhetorical devices are slanters. They slant you, turn you, bend or move you as well as twist and distort your understanding regarding a subject, issue, argument, or topic.

Language usually offers a choice of words when we want to say something. When we want to sugar coat something—sweet talk—happy speech—we use

EUPHEMISMS

Euphemisms use issue-distorting language. Euphemisms label or describe something by overly stating the positive and at once under stating the negative

The classic example of a euphemism is calling a used car a pre-owned car. It sounds better. Euphemisms affect our attitudes. Instead of saying torture—which is negative—called it "enhanced interrogation means," instead of spying say "intelligence mission," replace saying death, and say "passed on, " redefine tax hike by calling it "revenue enhancement," relable civilian casualties as "collateral damage" and describe a retreat as "strategic withdrawal"... and so on.

Euphemisms create a positive attitude about something—so that something is less distasteful, offense, touchy, or negative.

In modifying the scientific reports on the result of Global Warming significantly due to human activity, Philip Cooney, the chief of staff of the CEQ, edited the test to read that the scientific model simulations only "indicated" that there were "likely" changes as a result of human activity—hence a bit euphemistic and a bit of a weasler at once. He did so to lessen the negative implications of global warming or global wierding because the Bush Administration did not want the public or our politicians to be alarmed by the full implications of climate change. Obviously he intentionally used euphemisms in the hopes of pacifying people from what, factually, is a serious moral issue and a matter ultimately of our survival or at least the quality of life on earth for generations to come.

Opposite euphemisms are:

DYSPHEMISMS

Dysphemisms are used to create a negative attitude or feeling about something. Dysphemisms tone down the positive aspects of something and exaggerate the negative or unpleasant aspects of an issue or claim. Whereas "freedom fighter" is a euphemism for "rebel" or "guerrilla," the word "terrorist" is a dysphemism. Calling the Native Americans "savages" was a dysphemism. Thus, this dysphemism demonized and depersonalized the enemy. Calling your teacher a "monster" for requiring you to read the book is also a dysphemism.

Euphemisms and dysphemisms are often used in deceptive ways. But euphemisms can be helpful when one wants to modify the unpleasant aspects of something. Someone is not fat, but simply "pleasantly plump," or the car is not so banged up, but merely has "a few dents."

Further, unpleasant things are not always dysphemisms—neutral reports of horrid evil, injustice, tragedy, terror, and suffering do not count as dysphemistic rhetoric. If I say that there was genocide in Rwanda, I am not using a dysphemism. If I say that without government intervention the economy most likely would have collapsed, I am not using a dysphemism. And if I say we are going through a period of mass extinctions, I am also not using an dysphemism. These statements are strongly negative, but they are not exaggerations.

RHETORICAL DEFINITIONS AND RHETORICAL EXPLANATIONS

Rhetorical definitions use emotionally charged language, what we call loaded language, to express or elicit an attitude, positively or negatively, about something. Remember, the purpose of rhetoric is to slant you, to affect your emotions. Hence, defining abortion as the "murder of an unborn child" is rhetorical because the word "murder" and "child" are designed to invoke powerful emotions. Murder is very bad of course, especially when it is the "murder" of an innocent, helpless, cute "child." Defining abortion in this way stacks the decks for Pro-Life and against anyone who might be Pro-Choice or have a moderate, complex or nuanced position with respect to abortion. If you buy this rhetorical definition, in effect, you silence any serious discussion or debate over the real issue surrounding the abortion debate, i.e., the moral status of the fetus.

Hence, definitions can be used to persuade us in ways we may not be fully conscious of. Define a conservative as a "white supremacist," describe a liberal as "bleeding heart and tax and spend," call social reform and national health care as "socialism", "fascism," or a "national take over by Big Brother," or describe euthanasia as condoning "Nazi Death Camps" and you are slanting these definitions with the intention of achieving a derogatory and provocative impact.

Historically there have been plenty of examples of rhetorical definitions that took hold of people's beliefs and attitudes and resulted in irrational conduct. For instance, witch hunts, Satanism, anti-Semitism, the Nazi era, the Inquisition, the Maoist Cultural Revolution, and the McCarthy Era in the United States. Because language so profoundly informs what we believe it has the power to bless and dignify us or to turn us into the cruelest and sickest of animals as the ancient Greeks well knew.

Remember, language is power. If you can control the way something is defined, you can control the way people think about something. By contrast, if you do not work to define the situation for yourself, you may soon find that others will gladly define it for you. If you use the words liberal or socialism in an intentionally derogatory way—to evoke negative emotions—and you repeat it often enough, loudly enough, get enough people to accept your definition (and accept it with passion), then that definition appears to be true to many people even though it is a distorted and even purposefully misrepresentative definition. Control the discourse, define the situation, and you will have power, as both Mussolini and Hitler and others knew well. Define one policy after another as an aspect of the "war on terror" and this may very well invoke acceptance of what would otherwise be most unacceptable, such as torture. Add to this, by defining something as the "war on terror" you are appealing to an emotion rather than to terrorists themselves. Although emotions are not exactly something you can have a "war" on, by defining the situation in emotional terms this virtually assures an unending war.

Accordingly, if one wants to be open to all sides of an issue or policy, one must avoid rhetorical definitions which will slant the argument.

Rhetorical explanations are the same kind of slanting device as rhetorical definitions. He lost the fight because he was chicken—is a rhetorical explanation. This is not a rational explanation.

See if you can tell the difference between an explanation—and one that is rhetorical. Rhetorical explanations pop up everywhere in the media.

STEREOTYPES

When a speaker or writer lumps a group of individuals together under a slogan, description, category, cliché, or generalization (and especially when they use the word "the" to label the group generally), the result is a stereotype. Now, we all use stereotypes. But a stereotype is an image or word about a group of people, or even an individual person, based on little or no evidence and no discerning observation of individual differences. Stereotypes reduce people to things, to slogans. Stereotypes reify people. Stereotypes make judgments concerning these groups of individuals on the basis of ignorance, abstractions, simplifications, and prejudice. Stereotypes are lazy ways of viewing people and things.

There are stereotypes about women, gays, ethnic groups, people in religion or in politics, people with disabilities, people with short comings, and so on. Stereotypes often display contempt prior to investigation.

These are slanders and slanters. They are snap judgments. For example, if we use the dysphemism "right-wing extremist" to define a political candidate we are using a negative stereotype. Or we can create a positive stereotype by calling a political candidate a "gentleman." If one were to raise an issue about consumer oriented capitalism and the environment, one commentator could slant the issue positively by calling it freedom and a free market economy and then claim if you raised doubts about this that you were guilty of "leftist propaganda." By using the latter stereotype, he would thereby hush any debate.

Stereotypes are generalizations, abstractions. And they can be dangerous. Calling those outside your own religious denomination "the heathens" or "the infidel" or "the heretics" or "the enemy" has led to a great deal of bloodshed.

Stereotypes about women such as dumb blonde, soccer mom, earth mom, broad, and so on are emotional, not logical labels. Stereotypes can be annoying; they can be hurtful. Indeed, many stereotypes about women have been so culturally indoctrinated into people that they are unquestioned and presumed natural. Yet these stereotypes are often very harmful. Here stereotypes re-enforce oppression because, for instance, women are perceived as more emotional than logical. If your job or education requires that you be logical, analytical, scientific, or mathematically inclined you will be automatically branded as being incapable of the task. Further, if you prove you are in fact capable of the task, you will be labeled as masculine, disturbed, frigid, or even a dike (a dysphemistic stereotype).

An outspoken, independent or intellectual woman must be perceived as a lesbian and called dysphemistically a dike or she might be stereotyped as a "radical feminist" with the deliberate intention to taint the notion of feminism negatively. It is extremely doubtful that the person using these stereotypes is bothered to consider such a woman as full individual person. It is also unlikely that the person projecting stereotypes ever bothered to look up the philosophical definition of "radical feminist" to begin with. This is ironic because philosophically radical feminists actually place a great deal of emphasis on women's embodiment, motherhood, relationships, families, and reproductive issues. Now isn't that something! They don't burn their bras or even promote lesbian separatism! But the stereotype "radical feminist," by contrast, assumes these women instead to be men haters. Recall again that language is power and here we have a paragon instance of misogyny at work through a stereotype. Add to this that there are as many different kinds of feminist viewpoints as there are different kinds of philosophies and one might surmise that the use of stereotypes about women isn't simply oversimplification, it is stupidity.

It is, in addition, most likely that people using such stereotypes have never bothered to study feminism or to consider women's issues. If patriarchy works for you—you will want to reinforce it with stereotypes about women. You will also want to confuse women too about sexism, their own identities, and patriarchy. The same problems occur with racism although it is less openly discussed these days and even overtly denied while covertly and practically affirmed.

While stereotypes concerning women and racial minorities are often rebutted and have often gone underground, stereotypes concerning homosexuals are in some circles still out barking. Gays are considered effeminate, confused, mentally and sexually defiant, freaks, pedophiles, damned, and overall queers.

In these examples, stereotypes allow people to bracket others and to dehumanize them instead of evaluating a person on his or her character and merits. With this, women, Jews, minorities, and homosexuals can be depreciated rather than appreciated. Some of the greatest spiritual teachers in history have fought against the use of stereotypes. Stereotypes can be the dangerous toys of the immature, childish things we should outgrow.

Realize stereotypes have permitted people to go to war, to commit genocide, to torture, to enslave and so on. It's pretty easy to believe in stereotypes and to use them. Indeed, by saying your stereotypes often, loudly, and with passion, you stand the chance of convincing as many others as possible and thereby of preserving and promoting your sense of power and position. Accordingly, stereotypes can be enormously self-serving.

Once you have defined the discourse, in effect, you have the power ... if people buy into your stereotypes uncritically.

How do you feel about stereotypes that Americans are stupid? What do you think about religious stereotypes?

If you are a Christian, Hindu, Jew and a Muslim calls you an infidel—you probably won't like it. If you are a progressive, and someone calls you a commie, you might feel misunderstood, threatened, or dismissed. Senator Joe McCarthy in the early 1950's wiped out many people's careers by calling them communist and he silenced for several decades any rational, open discussion about Communism, Marxism, and Socialism. Indeed, students avoided Russian studies and learning the Russian language even though we were engaged in a prolonged and costly Cold War with Russia. Thus, stereotypes have produced enormous fear and even hysteria in the United States.

There are numerous cases of stereotypes used to justify war, terrorist attacks, etc. For instance, ironically, the *Koran* says all people of the Book and are NOT infidels. Indeed any moral religion does not fall under the label of infidel. But this simplistic, prejudice, ignorant, and historical stereotype allows one person to kill another, even other Muslims although this is expressly forbidden in the *Koran*. Or again, the Communists in Europe were very pro-democracy and were horrified with the results of the Russian Revolution. But they had to be oppressed by the power elite and this was done most effectively by Hitler's death camps.

Yes, people kill other people because of stereotypes. How easy is this? It is easy to bomb an abstraction called "the enemy." It is easy to blow up innocent "infidels" too. It was easy for the Hutus in Rwanda to exterminate eight hundred thousand to one million of their Tutsi neighbors and fellow citizens by labeling them "cockroaches." The Tutsi weren't people after all. They were infesting bugs. Hitler also made enormous use of stereotypes in order to massacre thirteen million Jews, Christians, Socialists, Communists, Slavs, gypsies, the disabled and the mentally retarded and of course anyone who protested his dictatorship and atrocities.

INNUENDO

Innuendos involve manipulating features of language. When we communicate we have certain expectations. We make certain assumptions. Not everything is always stated, sometimes things are implied. Hence, there are hidden meanings inside the words. When you teacher says everyone passed the test, she does not mean everyone in the world passed, only that everyone in that class passed. These expectations and assumptions help us fill the gaps in our communication.

Innuendos play on those assumptions. They get points across without explicitly making the point.

So when Hillary Clinton was asked if Obama was a Muslim—she said, "No—not as far as I know." It implied that since she does not know everything—Obama could be a Muslim—yet, explicitly she was denying that Obama is a Muslim.

Consider this statement:

- "Ladies and gentlemen, I am proof that there is at least one candidate in this race who does not have a drinking problem."

The speaker does not say that any opponent has a drinking problem, but we assume that the need to make this remark implies that there might be a candidate that in fact does have a drinking problem.

Hence, an innuendo enables us to insinuate something depreciatory about someone or something without really saying it.

- "My, Mary—you look good … eh … *today*."

Obviously, Mary has not looked good on other days.

Innuendos have many uses—and can be funny. Innuendos are clever techniques used by many comedians. Innuendos can, for example, be effective in communicating an interest in seduction. Through the use of innuendos one never mentions sex. Euphemisms too, like innuendos, can express discrete codes used to hint at a night of fertilizing the orchids, playing ball games, exploring the hidden cave, climbing the mountain, or visiting the Promised Land. Certain TV shows make ample use of innuendos and euphemisms like *Desperate House Wives*. If you get the innuendos and euphemisms you will find the show quite hilarious.

LOADED OR COMPLEX QUESTIONS

Another form of innuendo is a loaded or complex question. A loaded question makes unwarranted assumptions—"Have you stopped beating your wife?" The question seems to require a Yes or No answer but in fact entails a previous question—the assumption that in fact you ever beat your wife. Hence, a loaded question is not straightforward; it contains an assumption that is hidden but that one must implicitly agree to or acknowledge in order to answer the question. A loaded or complex question seems to ask for a Yes or No answer. But it traps you. No matter whether you answer the question Yes or No, such an acknowledgement commits the respondent to a position or a claim he or she would not have otherwise agreed to.

Complex questions cannot actually be answered Yes or No, although they try to pressure you into doing so, because complex questions entail a previous question you have not yet answered. By answering the complex question without being able to answer the previous question—you implicate yourself.

- Have you always loved to gamble?—assumes you loved to gamble.
- Where you out smoking pot again last night?—assumes you smoke pot.
- Have you stopped drinking?—assumes you drink.

The assumption is independent from whether or not you can answer the direct question yes or no. Hence, a loaded or complex question is not innocent.

Thus, in order to handle a complex or loaded question you need to ask yourself if the question contains hidden assumptions that force the respondent into an unacceptable situation.

WEASELERS

Weaselers are claims that hedge your bet. Weaselers insert words or phrases that water down the claim. Psychologically they fool you into believing the claim is strong, whereas the weaseler has weakened it. You just don't notice.

Weasel Words: Weaselers do what weasels. Weasels suck out the insides of eggs. Accordingly, weaselers suck out the substance of what appears on the surface to be a substantial claim. Specifically, weasel words make the claim in which it is used a vague claim while at least partially concealing the vagueness. "Help" functions in advertising as a weasel word. Once "help" is used to qualify a claim, the claim is diluted, and almost anything can be said after it. Accordingly, we are exposed to ads for products that "helps keep us young," "helps whiten your teeth" "helps prevent cavities," "helps prevent bad breath," "helps keep our houses germ free, " "helps stop," "helps prevent," "helps fight," "helps overcome," "helps you feel," "helps you look" and so on. Other weasel words include "looks." For instance, "makes your floor look like new." But your floor obviously is not new and they have made no real commitment to actually renewing it. Again, other weasel words include "virtual" or "virtually, "up to," "as much as." You may hear that a medicine "can provide relief for up to eight hours," but what the ad actually said is that the product may give no relief and if it does the relief could vary in length from a moment or two to anywhere up to 8 hours.

Weasel phrases are claims where one dilutes the claim and, effectively, hedges one's bet. But you are fooled into believing the claim is straightforward.

Weaselers protect the claim from criticism. Weaselers are often used in advertising. When you hear the words " helps to," "looks like," "up to," "seems like," "virtually new," "nearly new," "works like," "almost," "virtually eliminates," "works like," "in as much as," "insofar as," "is likely," "perhaps," "possibly," "maybe," and so on—you are hearing weaselers. Hence, weaselers also plant suggestions.

- Up to 50% off on a sale.
  —Check. Most items are probably not 50% off.

- Makes your car look virtually like new.
  —But your car is not new.
- Gets up to 35 miles a gallon.
  —Perhaps, if you were pushing your car down a hill.

Weaselers can be very tricky. They are designed to mislead you. Say most doctors or scientists agree upon something, but a few do not. You want to weasel this. To do so, you say some doctors or scientist disagree, even though you are only speaking for the 2% that disagree, you have succeeded in making the claims or beliefs of the other 98% of doctors or scientists less convincing.

Of course not every word or phrase that uses the aforementioned words are using weaselers. This is to say, a word that is a weaseler in one context is not a weaseler in another. In another context, it may convey important information. Weaseler words, like downplays, as we will see, are context-dependent.

So you are going to have to think about things. If someone says to you Dr. Smith may be lying, this need not be a case of weaseling. Phrases like "it is arguable that" and "it may well be that" may be legitimate—whereas phrases such as "some would say that" are more likely to be weaselers.

Simply watch for when these qualifying words turn up in claims, especially in advertising or when said by an interested party.

Again, it is a matter of awareness and practice. You will need to be able to assess the context in order to judge.

A classic example of the use of phrases that involve weaselers is the statement that "four out of five dentists surveyed recommend sugarless gum—to their patients that chew gum." Here we have two weaselers.

The word "surveyed" doesn't tell the criteria used in choosing the dentist surveyed. What kind of a survey was this? And the second weaseler is "for their patients who chew gum. " The ad does not claim that most dentists believe chewing sugarless gum is good for a patient's teeth or better than chewing no gum chewing at all. The ad sounds like you should chew gum (and then of course sugarless gum). It sounds like most dentists recommended chewing gum. If you believe this, you have been weaseled.

DOWNPLAYERS

Downplayers are not put downs, negative comments, or insults. Downplayers are not dysphemisms. Rather downplays are ways of minimizing something. Downplayers reduce the importance of something. Downplays make something or someone look less significant or important. "Don't pay attention to what Dr. Roth says in class, she's just another liberal." Not only does this use a stereotype, the phrase "just another" downplays.

Words that are most often used as downplayers are "mere," "merely," "only," "allegedly," "so-called," "in as much as," "assumedly," "but", "still", "nevertheless," "nonetheless," "it seems," and "seemingly ." If I say the bailout for the banks was a *mere* 12 trillion dollars—you might wonder how 12 trillion dollars could be so mere. Don't worry. The bailout for Wall Street was only 12 trillion dollars, and so what?

Of course downplayers can play off other words to achieve the effect of down playing or minimizing.

- She got her "degree" from a correspondence school.
- Obviously, she did not get a real degree.

- She got her degree from a "university."
- But it was hardly what we normally mean by a university.

- Pete "borrowed" Hal's umbrella—and Hal has not seen it since.
- Pete didn't borrow the umbrella at all; he stole it.

- Of course George Bush "won" the 2000 Presidential Election.
- This implies Bush didn't really win the election, when in fact he did, although the means and methods for such a win are surely in dispute.

These words play down the importance of the subject.

Many conjunctions such as "nevertheless," "however," "still," and "but" as mentioned can also be used as downplayers.

"Those 3,000 deaths in the chemical plant in India were a terrible tragedy of course, however, we must remember the plant is an integral part of the 'green revolution' that has helped to feed millions."

This statement downplays the tragedy, and expresses the speaker's point of view, which miminizes the tragedy in relation to other objectives.

Realize, you will have to think about the context because sometimes downplayers are used subtlety. Plus, words that are downplayers in one context, are not downplays in another context.

If I say Robert weighs only 105 pounds, this is not a downplayer. (Unless Robert is a cat or rabbit.)

If I say Lester weighs only 350 pounds, this is a downplayer. (Unless Lester is a hippo or elephant.)

Remember, rhetorical devices manipulate language. We cannot escape them, but we need to be aware of them. By manipulating language, rhetorical devices manipulate the way we think about things, our attitudes, feelings, images, actions and, finally, of course, our society.

HORSE LAUGH/RIDICULE/SARCASM

The rhetorical device we call a horse laugh includes all kinds of sarcasm.

Ridicule is powerful. It can be funny and clever. Nevertheless, it should be remembered that just because someone ridicules another person does not mean that the other person's positions or claims should also be dismissed.

A horse laugh gets us to laugh. Whole books, movies, and TV entertainment shows are filled with hilarious horse laughs and sarcasm. A lot of us appreciate dry or dark humor and tongue-in-cheek wit. Shows like John Stewart's *The Daily Show* are witty, thought-provoking, and informative. Shows like *Saturday Night Live* at times reach a high level of ridicule, sarcasm, and of course humor. Certain film directors, like Woody Allen, Mel Brooks, and the Monty Python movies, are stylistically filled with horse laughs. And the movie *Doctor Strangelove* is a classic spoof on the Cold War. But as critical thinkers you should be able to tell the difference between a thoughtful argument—and ridicule or sarcasm.

Of course, for some people horse laughs are offensive. Offense of cultural norms and twists on social stereotypes is simply one art form in this vast array of language usage that began with the early Greeks in the play *The Clouds* which satirized Socrates.

Learning how to write using rhetorical devices is important. It can also be a lot of fun. Many excellent writers use a wide variety of rhetorical devices in numerous contexts. Hence, it is important to recognize them.

HYPERBOLE

Another commonly used rhetorical device is hyperbole. A hyperbole is an exaggeration, an overstatement. It is extravagant, excessive. One is hyperbolic when one expresses things in the extreme.

Hyperbole's can be used with dysphemisms.

"Parents who are strict with their children are fascists."

Hyperboles are used with rhetorical definitions, rhetorical explanations, and rhetorical analogies. Hyperbole's can also be used in ridicule.

Hence, hyperboles are quite common place.

Hyperboles are so common place that we may accept them unconsciously without realizing that a more moderate claim is closer to the truth. Thus, while hyperboles can be used playfully, in some context, they can also be provocative and troublesome.

PROOF SURROGATES

A surrogate is not real. For instance, a surrogate mother is not a real mother. She is a substitute. An expression or claim used to suggest that there is evidence or authority for a statement, assertion or belief that does not actually cite such evidence or authority is a proof surrogate. Sometimes people hint that there is proof for their claims such as "We have every reason to believe," "our sources tell us," "informed sources say," "we have heard that," "it's obvious that," "studies show," "it was disclosed to us that," "we have learned that," "we have testimony that," and so on. None of these claims explicitly tells us what sources, what authority. Without a context, such assertions are meaningless. They can even be dangerous if you are taken in to believe something without really knowing the evidence, proof, facts, authority, witnesses, etc. of the claims being made.

People use proof surrogates to get you to believe something without actually providing proof. People can be taken in by proof surrogates easily because people tend to trust others, especially people in power or positions of authority. But using proof surrogates, rather than real proofs, has consequences, including to one's credibility.

General Collin Powel was taken in by proof surrogates in his speech before the UN on why the United States needed to invade Iraq. We now know there were no WMD in Iraq, but a series of proof surrogates and some very non-credible biased parties were perfectly willing to mislead Powel with devastating consequences to his credibility and career as well as to our country and millions of Iraqis.

Obviously proof surrogates can be very dangerous. They can be used by people with agendas. They can be used as propaganda. And when people fail to be critical thinkers, proof surrogates can have tragic consequences.

RHETORICAL ANALOGIES

An analogy is when we say something is like, similar to, compares with, is a metaphor for or a simile for, or that something looks like or appears similar to something else. Whereas a rhetorical definition says something is or equals X—a rhetorical analogy says X is like Y. Thus all metaphors depend on analogies.

Rhetorical analogies are often used to substitute for arguments. Instead of using facts or being precise or accurate, by using a rhetorical analogy, an emotional comparison, one can be persuasive.

Rhetorical analogies can be used with dysphemisms, hyperboles, and sarcasm. Hence, they can be funny, dry, offensive, insulting, misleading, etc.

"Having kids is like having a bowling alley installed in your brain."

This is funny. It is of course a rhetorical analogy. Obviously, a bowling alley is not literally in your head.

Accordingly, we often use analogies. Analogies can be neutral. But analogies can also be rhetorical when they are designed to use rhetorical force, i.e., to be psychologically persuasive.

You can use analogies in arguments. You can use rhetorical analogies to assist your argument. You can use analogies in good writing. But when the analogies are rhetorical, you must bear in mind that they are not facts or proofs. Their aim is to persuade you, to slant you positively or negatively about something.

The Voucher System for LA

DETERMINE WHETHER THE FOLLOWING ARE:

(a) no slanter	(b) euphemism	(c) dysphemism	(d) stereotype
(e) rhetorical analogy or analogy	(f) rhetorical definition	(g) rhetorical explanation	(h) innuendo
(i) hyperbole	(j) ridicule, horses laugh	(k) weasler	(l) downplayer
(m) proof surrogate	(n) loaded/complex question		

The LA Public School District has got to be the worse school district in California (1) _____. It is run by a bunch of fat-cat (2) _____ administrators who rule the school district like Neo-Stalists where only party members benefit (3) _____. Teachers get tenured within 2 years; and some teachers are not even required to have credentials. (4) _____. Then they overcrowd the classrooms with snotty, swearing chip-on-their shoulder bad ass kids (5)_____ from dysfunctional and derelict families (6)____and expect the kids to get "educated" (7)_____ when they would rather text message and listen to Hip Hop music. When you add to that that many of these kids are from illegal immigrants who cannot read in Spanish very well, let alone English—you can start to understand why the *LA Times* said residents in LA had only (8)_____ a 53% illiteracy rate. (Obviously not good for the *LATimes* subscription rate!)

But the *LA Times* has gone further in pointing out that since a mere (9) _____ 80% of students are inadequately educated, by 2030, 80% of the population in LA will live in absolute destitution and squalor (10)_____ working minimum wage jobs probably without health insurance or benefits—effectively they will be wage-slaves. By contrast, the 20% who worked hard to get educated and make a success out of their lives will live in luxury gated communities (11) _____. We will have a two class system—with the vast majority living like lower level hicks at the material bottom of the Platonic realm of forms—and the small minority living in the higher, celestial realm of the perfect forms (12)_____.

But, we have every reason to believe (13)_____ that it might be possible (14)_____ for things not to turn out this way. Not in the sense that the Religious Right

(15) _____ believe: that Jesus will come and save the little literalist pious peons who cannot read, write, or think (16)_____ and who think the presence of Dinosaurs and Wooly Mammoths was simply God's loving way of determining who would make man's best friend (17)_____ from the utter exploitation and domination (18)_____ of the upper class elite snobs (19)_____. Instead, there is some movement a foot to begin a Voucher Program, where even lower and middle class students can afford to go to private, partnership, or charter schools—escaping the hellish underworld of LA Unified School District (20)_____.

The Voucher system allows families to receive checks for their children's education. Parents can then select from any school of their choice—where they would like their children to attend. This introduces competition in the school system. Schools that can compete will attract students, and better teachers; schools that are failing, will have to clean up their act or will simply fail. Because per student, private education is less expensive than public education, with the Voucher system, many parents may opt for private schools. This will actually free tax payer dollars for education to be directed to help clean up failing schools unless their big money Administrators (21)_____are willing to find themselves (and their faculty) in the sewers living with the Jesus-loves-me not yet ruptured illiterates (22)_____. Of course the Administrators may just set out to totally wreck (23) _____the entire LA Unified School District. While lining their pockets they could allege that they might be better able to "educate" (24)_____ if we would just fork over more money. Well, now their system of education after all does "work." (25)_____. ...if you are looking for truck drivers, welfare moms, drug pushers, sweat shop slaves, custodial and security services, prison guards, trash collectors, hamburger flippers (26)_____ and hard working Se Hablo Español green thumbs (27)_____you can definitely see that. But modern society needs more than this to manage, and more than contented Rednecks (28)_____ as well who figure a 6 pack and joint can substitute for the rapture (29)_____. So why keep spending more money on a failing educational system? (30)_____ Why not hold the "Pros" (31)_____accountable? After all, they are supposed to be competent—in many regards (32)____.But again, these "so called" (33)_____educators are the very ones opposing the Voucher system. They would then have to get results. They would have to sit down with parents and students and make sure that Jose could read and Kenisha could do her multiplication tables. If the kids cannot do this, the way things are now, the Administrators keep their cushy jobs—and fewer and fewer people will read the *LA Times*. Get it?

Washington "Health Care"

- The following essay makes use of sarcasm and a number of rhetorical devices. It is an example of op-ed writing that might appear in a newspaper or magazine or even a book.
- See if you can identify the various rhetorical devices used and if you can recognize the sarcasm and horse laughs. Contrast that with the factual and serious statements that are also made.
- Why might one want to write about this topic with sarcasm?

The United States of America is the only industrialized nation in the world—other than South Africa—lacking a national health insurance program. (Well, South Africa has a "tradition" of "caring" about the majority of its people—so what's new?) As a result, it is claimed that some 48–50 million Americans lack health insurance altogether and another 68 million are under insured. Add to this the roughly 15 million who are registered as unemployed and about the same number who are under employed, temporary employees, free lance workers, the self-employed, small business owners, and those entering the work force—who do not qualify for unemployment benefits—and those whose unemployment benefits have run out—and the number of people who may have difficulty obtaining or affording health insurance drastically increases. Then add all those who have a pre-existing conditions—a little high blood pressure, or cholesterol, a family history of diabetes, or perhaps a DNA test showing that perhaps someday you might get failing pancreas or a slipped disk —whatever—and you cannot afford most likely to pay to be in the system. You're out of luck in more ways than one.

Yet the United States of America spends 16% of its Gross National Product on health care—and this is increasing and increasing and increasing. It's a very hungry beast. Why I'm even sure that conservatives—such as David Brooks—would agree with me on this one. Now 16%, then 20%, and soon enough 23% of the GNP—a real slippery slope in rising health care cost that would choke up any honest conservative or liberal. (Another 20% of our GNP is made by our wonderful, oblivious- to- moral- hazard, greed gorging, dark side financial institutions that devour like termites the foundations of the economy.) Conclusion: the worst of all possible systems. No hyperbole intended. Simply put, Voltaire's Penglos in reverse. (I refer to the French often in this essay—be forewarned.) For all this money, the United States ranks 31st in life expectancy (tied with Chile and Kuwait); we rank 37th in infant mortality and 34th in maternal mortality. A child in the United States is two-and-a-half times more likely to die before age 5 than in Sweden or Singapore. A woman in America is 11 times more likely to die in childbirth than a woman in Ireland.

Perhaps pregnant woman in America simply don't drink enough Guinness beer, you think? Or are these results likely due to bad genes in America? But then Canadians do better than us too—and they are rather similar to us in looks, history, diet, air quality, ancestors, and language. And we have better weather. Further, of 19 developed countries, the United States ranked last in preventable deaths. So it just can't be due to genes, beer, or the weather.

Now health care is a need, not a commodity. It's like saying you have to buy your body—it is not ready made through you parents and nature—and perhaps ultimately God. No—you buy your body or sell it. Buying your body—most legal—selling it, legal with exceptions. Facts. Tens of thousands of Americans die every year needlessly due to lack of proper medical care, or endure chronic illnesses without treatment, or lack preventative care that would help them contribute to society or fail to get needed care that would help them sustain and support their families, etc. For example, the cost of complicated and premature child births and unhealthy babies adds tens of billions of dollars to the cost of our health care system due to lack of pre-natal care. Pre-natal care, by contrast, would cost on average around $1,200 per child in a clinic. And it's humane to care about babies and mommies. Everyone started there. Nevertheless, the United States of America ranks 27th in the world with respect to life expectancy and infant mortality—next to Slovenia. Now Slovenia is a beautiful country no doubt. But historically, it has had some very hard times. So perhaps you could say America has the best health care system of 3rd world countries. Then you would not be deluding yourself.

Nevertheless, Washington cannot really reform health care. Certain people say, that would be "socialism"—and we cannot have that. By their standard, the police and fire departments are socialistic, so too the public school system (see what socialism gets you?)—why even most of our parks are socialistic.

So let us privatize Smokey the Bear. See the problem? Labeling something socialist is not helpful, but it sure works as a smoke screen. Health care is a need—a basic need—but with enough smoke it looks like a political agenda by the left, those darn bleeding heart, radical, socialist, commie-loving liberals and their extreme leftist propaganda. Why these liberals (i.e., socialists) are as bad as the scientific community and their conspiracy to teach atheistic Darwinism and claim that climate change is a fact, and we have a moral obligation to protect nature and future generations. But what future generations? After all, for the Moral Majority, the wingers, the Free Marketeers, the end-of-time Rapturists, and the Pious Pentecosts, the earth has only been around for some 6,000 years and so we owe nothing to the future—and very little to the past. By contrast, those godless alarmists, who think facts matter, are the real beast of Armageddon. If they don't already you want to scream, rant, and pull out your revolver, a national health insurance program will. Why according to some higher ups, the result of a national health insurance plan would be Nazi death camps. Then again, Nazi death camps are a more cost effective way of killing people than our current costly private health care system. So perhaps there is a point to their point. With this, the argument from outrage is sure to incinerate facts, documents, and issues as well as well as those bleeding heart liberals.

Back to our issue. Given the extreme power of the left—watch your wallet. Taxes and taxes. Right? That's the wingers mantra. Nonetheless, although the majority of Americans support at least some form of a public option health insurance policy—even with a slight increase in taxes (although a single payer system actually reduces costs)—Washington will not. Washington is bought by super capitalism.

This is the system. This is the beast. There is a price tag on your health, your life, your babies, your family, your peace of mind. This is our capitalism. You pay to play. You don't, you die. Or, if you don't die yet—you can file medical bankruptcy and do a foreclosure at the same time. Free at last!

Put mildly and euphemistically, our current health care system is by way of rhetorical definition a form of Social Darwinism laughing its hyena face as it chows down the carcass of the social contract. The market after all will define survival of the fittest, literally. Praise almighty Ayn Rand.

But wait! Sweden, Norway, Finland, Denmark, England, Scotland, Ireland, Germany, Poland, Spain, France, Japan, Australia, New Zealand, Singapore, South Korea, Taiwan—and so on—are our friends right? But they all have single payer systems. So they must in fact be socialist! Jee wiz, then we did not "win" the cold war after all, now did we? Gosh, another smokescreen, who would have thought?

France, best health care system in the world, has a single payer system (socialism?). But France's system costs half as much per person as our system. Why even a good capitalist seeking nothing but profit can understand saving health care cost on employees—you might think. Further, in France, if you want additional health insurance you can always buy private health insurance as well. Yep. (Likewise you have private options in England and Germany.) If you happen not only to be French, but the more capitalist elite—and most French consider themselves elite—you can buy additional health insurance for extras. Tres Jolie! Translate: WOW! No reason for the current multi-billion dollar for profit private health insurance companies in the USA to threaten Congress that a public option (not to mention a single payer system) will undermine and destroy the so-called best private health insurance system in the world. Actually, there are more doctors in private practice and more private hospitals in many countries with national health insurance—all competing for patients. Yes, for Adam Smith, the good side of capitalism, competition. Capitalism—but who would have thought?

A mommy in France? You get pre-natal care and a lot more than that! Once Jacque or Françoise, Bernadette or Antoinette, Louise or Pierre are born you also get regular meetings with your doctor and health care workers to assist you in baby health issues, including nutrition. Even more, in many of these capitalist countries you get paid family leave to look after your little ones. Very pro-family, you think? Why busy mom, some systems have people come by to help you do the laundry and do a bit of baby-sitting for you—so you can take a sanity break. After all, your baby is not yet a Robber Barron capable of self-sufficient Social Darwinism and you are still human and not a robot.

Don't want a baby? There's lots of assistance to help you there too. For instance, there are sex education classes. Children in Sweden take sex education classes. In turn, this helps them by preventing the spread of socially transmitted diseases, abortions and unwanted pregnancies. Knowing something about sex probably also adds to their peace of mind. You'll know that you do not need to weep hysterically when your husband takes a piss—he is not flushing little babies down the toilet. You'll know it's okay to clean your private body parts to prevent disease even though that does mean you will have to touch yourself. You'll know that a tubal pregnancy will kill you, that you need to see a doctor, and that the required surgery does not constitute an abortion since the embryo didn't make it into the launch pad to begin with. And you'll know that while there are only certain times when a woman can get pregnant that time is not defined as early withdrawal. Where are the Pro-Lifers when we need them?

Now of course the French have a thing for "love." (So do others.) So oops, "love" happened when you fell asleep on the sunny beach of Nice (when you were bare breasted and had had too much good wine and food) and you are not quite sure about how Tres Jolie you feel about that moment of "love." Okay, France will give you a wake up pill from your dreams—which comes with a couple of additional therapy sessions to help you deal with reality and not just dreams in the future. It's ultimately called prevention. You might not make the same mistake.

Now I realize America has not always felt cozy with the French. After all, the Native Americans liked the French, way back when … and we didn't like them red-skinned savages (but we sure liked their land). But still we could learn something from the French—Julia Child did. But will we? (The French have a few other good ideas like philosophy, red wine, literature, fashion, perfume, banking reform and even energy independence (so do others).

Will we learn from the French—or any of our "fake" capitalist friends out there? Apparently not.

We have our vision of Capitalism. They have theirs. They have French Fries. We, being exceptional, have Freedom Fries. So the story goes.

By Freedom Fries we mean private health insurance, etc. We mean private about everything, anything—if we can only get it. But wait. Is the system so private? So capitalistic? So free? Congress has ingeniously come up with a stipulative definition of private health insurance and freedom. You must buy it, or else. If you cannot afford private health insurance, then you will be able to write it off your taxes so other tax payers will indirectly pick up your bills. Or, we will just keep adding up to the public deficit—that will grow to many times more than the annual GNP. And then of course, one way or another, that will kill the beast, I mean, that is, the government.

But—hold your breath! (We may not resuscitate.) Or, hold your bladder (we have meds for that). Might there be a contradiction here? We don't want national health insurance (that would be socialist—remember?), but we are perfectly willing to subsidize private health insurance at tax payers expense. Socialist Capitalism. Well, we do that already with so many other businesses (banks, farms, insurance companies, oil, coal, cars, not to mention the military complex, etc.)—so what's new?

And that is the plan! Yep. That's the system. Bought and paid for by special interest groups—over all of the American people. Tax payers, the self-employed, small business owners, and so on, hold on to your appendix or kidneys—as soon everything will be open for trade on the Stock Market. Freedom Fries indeed! How yummy.

So let's ignore the human suffering that results from not having a national health insurance plan—as Jesus ignored the suffering of others—as, after all, you stop suffering when you die. And let us let the very few people who profit to the extreme from the private health care insurance system—the financial system—the energy system—and so on—rape and reap.

Lacking a national health insurance program is bad for the American people. It is bad for business. It is bad for the dedicated people in the health care field. And, ironically, it ultimately makes American Capitalism unsustainable. But it will be a slow death, with death of course being the ultimate cure. Death is after all a 100% proven cure even for chronic back pain. Indeed, forget diet, exercise, rest, or costly medical care—the ultimate cure for all pain is of course death. Freud knew this so he kept smoking that cigar that was only a cigar. (Do you suppose he was repressing something?)

But of course this is not a painless death. The injustices of our private health care system lie all around us. Nonetheless, for the lobbyists for private health insurance and pharmaceutical companies the uninsured are simply like annoying beavers worth more for their pelts than for their lives. So the beast of the private health insurance system—and its addiction to huge profits (like other institutions in our system)—will not give up. It will kill the beast—government, society, and eventually you—and then it will rise even higher, fatter, and more costly. Americans, which beast will you back? Who is your beast of beasts? Having a sense of humor, I might be able to see that the concept of the beast is an open interpretation from the *Revelation of John*. Who would have thought?

The High and Low Tides of American Education

WRITING WITH ANALOGIES AND METAPHORS

- A Considerable amount of good writing and arguing involves the effective use of analogies (both neutral and rhetorical) along with the use of metaphors. In this essay, identify the analogies and metaphors.

Warren Buffett once famously snapped: "Only when the tide goes out do you find out who is not wearing a bathing suit." (http://www.nytimes.com/2009/04/22/opinion/22friedman.html?em) This applies to companies and financial institutions as we are witnessing today. The tide is going out and several major companies, financial, and insurance institutions appear to be naked. Economic bubbles are like the high tide. They hide the rocks, reefs, garbage, and slimy sea weeds of bad loans, mismanagement, greed, corruption, and incompetence in corporate America. The tide rose with easy credit and when the bubble burst and the tide went out, what was revealed were numerous weaknesses. It wasn't just that economic fundamentals were faltering in manufacturing, science, technology, health care, energy conservation and public transportation, and infrastructure. It also revealed that we had fallen behind in education and that the sea bed was awash of broken sea shells, polluted sea urchins, and disappearing coral. We had fallen way behind in K-12 education and to a great extent in many areas of higher education, and it was costing us. In the 1950s and 1960s, according to the study, "The Economic Impact of the Achievement Gap in America's Schools," by the consulting firm McKinsey, the United States was the economic leader of the world and in K-12 education. In the 1970s and 1980s we continued but to a lesser degree. We had fallen behind per capita in high school graduates and quality. For example, the SAT scores were "normalized" 50 points lower in the early 1970s. In reality, we had dumbed down, but it was dressed up to look like all was okay. "Re-adjusting" SAT scores was like the temporary fix of a Botox treatment.

As a result, the U.S. ranked 25th out of the 30 industrialized nations in math and 24th in science in the 2006 Program for International Student Assessment. While American children in fourth grade still did well on global tests, they began to really lag behind the longer they remained in school. Put differently, the recipe "cooks" fast—first get the students hooked on Big Macs and soda, TV and video games, then bake for several years, and then start the heavier stuff—from pot to porn to top it off. Finally, remove before graduation. Result, minimum wage workers—who are too lazy to vote—and too illiterate to read. Missed a few? Simply re-toss and re-cycle in the state university system—where 65%-70% of faculty are part-time instructors—with virtually no rights and often no health insurance or benefits. Further, these instructors, by necessity, usually hold down several jobs. Now pepper this with the fact that the competent faculty who manage to stay a few years still are at risk of no real commitment from their universities and colleges. And to put salt on the wounds, make sure the students know that probably they will not see their teachers in a few years—that teachers are plastic wrap—hence, disposable. Don't worry about "the environment." Add oil by making sure that instructors know that if they don't grade inflate—so they can get great student evaluations and make their students look better—their careers are absolutely terminal as Provost and Deans are upset with attrition and obsessed with student evaluations. And now add vinegar that unlike other nations, Americans do not feel a great deal of respect for the highly educated unless one makes a lot of money, which most teachers of course do not. Hence, many Americans cannot understand why one would study Aristotle or literature rather than be a Wall Street day trader or a real estate agent.

The full extent of the crisis is most evident in the Golden State, California. Once ranked the Number One and Number Two best public higher education system in the country, the California higher education system (not to mention K-12) is now ranked at the bottom for overall funding for education and nearly at the bottom on achievement tests. Yet California educates 1 out of 9 children in America. Tens of thousands of K-12 teachers were given their pink slips with the economic low tide, and tens of thousands of students are being denied access to the public higher education in Community Colleges, the California State University system, and the University of California system. And the cost of going to a CSU or UC campus has dramatically risen.

The State has finally crashed into the ocean, but not yet because of the Big One. Rather, the eroding of the system took decades until it finally became an all-out disaster. It started with Proposition 13 which fixed property taxes at low rates—property taxes which had been funding K-12 education. That meant education was no longer sufficiently funded through controllable property taxes, but instead was dependent on the state. The state's tax system in turn was based on boom/bust cycles with there being more busts than booms. Time and again the state cut additional programs, including the additional English language assistance for students that blast California like the Santa Ana winds. Finally, as the recent tides retreated back and back the Golden state had simply ran out of "gold." This exposed a shocking weakness in the entire state system that had faults as big as the San Andreas plus. Every community is California is affected.

Needed programs throughout the system and especially education were and are being chopped down and burnt, deforesting the once-proud system for the people, leaving education looking as dry and barren as Death Valley in summer. California is de-braining itself; with respect to education it's "chop of their heads" as teachers flee the state. Put simply, the tide went out leaving almost nothing for the boat to float on.

As for K-12, as many as 50% of students in the Los Angeles Unified School District fail to graduate from high school and that problem is epidemic—and not due to the Swine Flu. Further several CSU campuses have 70-80% attrition rates, a 4 year college degree now takes at least 5, and many programs are being terminated by the Gov. Terminator.

Effectively, this is also happening during the Great Recession when millions are out of work and might well want to be in school upgrading themselves so that they can swim rather than sink in today's economy.

Congress and Obama know there is a crisis—affecting many states—as the economic lotus have been devouring everything green. Millions of kids in modern suburban schools don't realize how far behind they are. Of course you cannot tell that to the kids, that would be politically incorrect, it would undermine the notion of social promotion and it might force the unions to require teacher accountability. Wait! Why not tell the kids they need to read books, poetry, listen to classical music, study science, geography, math, art, learn a foreign language, and study history, plus develop critical reasoning skills? Surely we cannot outsource all jobs, and surely even the wealthiest can understand that they may need a nurse or a bridge or a nutritionist someday. Surely we are not yet that braindead. Or are we? Consequently, we have the great education-gate cover up—perpetuated by administrators, unions, and politicians with race to the bottom policies!

It is not that we are failing across in every program or in every state. There are many exciting education innovations in America today — from new modes of teacher compensation (where teachers can earn around $125,000 per year by also participating in school district administration) to charter, voucher, or partnership schools, and so on, scattered around the country. These new innovations are showing real improvements based on better methods, principals, teachers, and higher standards. And even President Obama was willing to consider, however modestly, vouchers—(unfortunately, an otherwise Conservative movement because the Conservative Base often wants religion (theirs)—tossed into the recipe.) The problem is that these achievements are too scattered like oases in the desert — leaving all kinds of achievement gaps between whites, African-Americans, Latinos and *different income levels*. Of course family involvement is also crucial in education: a family that reads breeds readers, a family that expects achievement blooms achievers—no matter what their race or neighborhood. A family that does not value education probably is sentencing junior to a poor job, financial and family problems—sometimes gangs and crime—and even a shorter life expectancy! All of which are far more costly to the system than a decent education. Thus, it is the task of the school district to educate the parents on how important it is for junior to learn to read and go to the library and not just play video games and send text messages.

And why is this so urgent? Several reasons. First, the Baby Boomers that managed to get a decent education before the drought hit education, will soon be going into retirement and have not been reproduced. You cannot harvest if you have not planted. Second, China, India, and other nations are educating more engineers, scientists, and so on than the United States. China may thus become more inventive and increasingly able to compete and become the world's next superpower leaving the United States a pale, crippled, and speech-impaired dwarf. Third, people attracted to careers in K-12 education currently represent the bottom one-third of college students. Compare this with Finland which has the highest educational standards worldwide. There teachers are paid well and required to have at least an MA in some discipline in order to teach. Consequently our children here are falling behind the longer they remain prisoners of our current educational system because many of their teachers, especially in high school, themselves cannot perform above an 8th or 10th grade level in reading or math and would be better paid if they worked for the prison system directly than in an academic one. Finally, our low tide education is actually very costly to the United States as a whole. For instance, for every dollar spent on education in the California State University system, the state over time receives back $17 in revenue; for every dollar spent on the California Community College system, the state receives back $16 in revenue. Or again, the failure of our national educational standards since the 1980s can be compared to the results we could have achieved if we had not let the London Bridge of education all fall down. Suppose, the United States had fought back against lagging student standards and instead muscled up to set higher benchmarks of performance? According to McKinsey, the United States G.D.P. in 2008 would have been between $1.3 trillion and $2.3 trillion ***higher***. If we had closed the racial achievement gap of minority student performance so that they caught up with white students by 1998, G.D.P. in 2008 would have been between $310 billion and $525 billion higher. If the gap between low-income students and the rest had been narrowed, G.D.P. in 2008 would have been $400 billion to $670 billion higher. So education pays.

This is not the fault of the students. We spend more on the prison system in the state of California, for example, than we do on the entire CSU and UC system combined and we spend more on the interest on bonds alone per year as well. My goodness, Charles Dickens, wouldn't this be a story? Oh. I forgot. Students cannot read. Yet the students and their parents are not oblivious to the problem given the high drop out and attrition rates. Many are of course frustrated and want reform. Nevertheless, to reverse this trend will require an all-out fitness program of moral authority and leadership determined to reform education immediately. Of course, once one has gotten flabby it is difficult to shape up and putting education on a starvation diet only slows the metabolism down even further.

Now, there is hope. There are some new life guards and fitness trainers showing up. President Obama recognizes that we urgently need to invest the money and energy to take those schools and practices that are working from islands of excellence to all the land. But we need to do it with the sense of urgency and follow-through that many Americans, already dumbed down, are unaware of.

So the question is, will we act or will we be so virtually self-deluded as to believe that a nationwide recovery of our educational system needs only wait until real Martians show up and advise Irving Stone on how to put together the best Star Wars flick with minimum wage, illiterate workers?

Surely, as the tide goes out revealing the serous weakness in education, some children will yell "the Emperor has no clothes" and Americans will wake up to the fact we spent several decades de-robing ourselves and our now down to thongs and in saggy shape. Hardly the way one thinks of California dreaming.

Printed by Libri Plureos GmbH in Hamburg, Germany